THE COMPLETE CHIHUAHUA

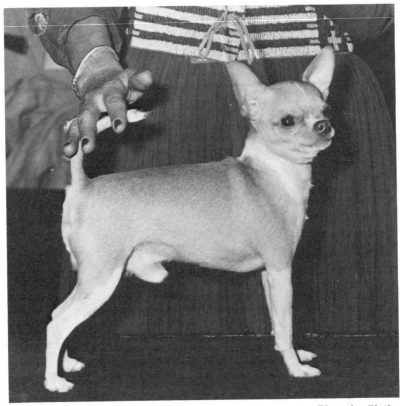

CH. TEJANO TEXAS KID, the foremost Best in Show Chihuahua of all time with 15 all-breed wins. Shown in the mid-1950s, Texas Kid was owned by Mr. and Mrs. Bob Roberts of San Antonio, Texas, and handled by Clara Alford.

The Complete

CHIHUAHUA

by

Rosina Casselli
Milo Denlinger
Elsworth Howell
Rev. Russell E. Kauffman
Dr. A. C. Merrick
Mrs. Anna B. Vinyard
James Watson

Illustrated

Fourth Edition, Sixth Printing

1983

HOWELL BOOK HOUSE INC.

230 Park Avenue

New York, N. Y. 10169

Le Gate's Parcee Rara Chico
Owner: The Ted Le Gates,
Watonga, Oklahoma

Table of Contents, Part 1

Table of Contents, Part 2

GENERAL CARE AND TRAINING OF YOUR DOG

THURMER'S CHI CHI
Owned by Mrs. Herbert Beck
Silver Spring, Md.

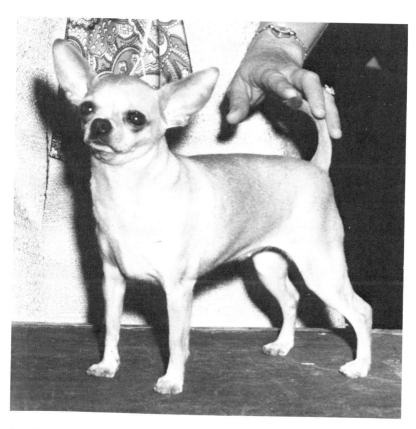

CH. HURD'S HONEY BEE, the top winning Chihuahua of 1969 (Phillips System). At mid-1970 her record included 2 Bests in Show, 2 Chihuahua Specialty Bests of Breed and 11 Toy Group Firsts. By King's Bounty ex Ch. Hurd's Bit O'Honey, she was bred by Max E. Hurd, president of the Chihuahua Club of America, and co-owned by Mr. Hurd and Teddye Dearborn.

CH. DARTAN'S BLAZON DRAGAN, red fawn with white blaze and markings, weighing 3 pounds. Blazon made his debut at six months of age at the 1968 Chihuahua Club of America Specialty, and was placed to Winners Dog for 5-point major by the English judge, Mrs. Thelma Grey. Bred by the Delaneys, and owned by Edward and Kaye Dragan of Detroit.

CH. CHAR-ELL'S EL DORADO OF DARTAN, Best in Show at the Motor City Specialty in Detroit in 1969, BOV at the Milwaukee Specialty 1969 and 1970, and Best Stud Dog at the Chihuahua Club of America Specialty 1970. Bred by the Delaneys, and owned by Charles and Jewell Gonic.

Foreword

This popular book on one of the world's most popular breeds is now in its fifth edition. The measure of its success derives from its acceptance by the proponents of this Lilliputian dog, a giant in character yet the smallest of all breeds ever developed by man. For many years the Chihuahua has ranked among the highest in the canine hit parade determined by pure-bred dog registrations.

This new edition carries forward from the peerless lore and early history of the breed to its latest winners including those of the great Westminster Kennel Club at Madison Square Garden in 1971. Its material on early and recent bloodlines constitutes priceless information for breeders. Mrs. Vinyard's chapter on Mexico contributes a fascinating account of the tiny dog's quality and future in the country of its origin. The compilation of outstanding winners for the last ten years provides a useful record in the breed's most recent history.

The scores of pictures, many of unique historical value and others of new champions, offer a magnificent photo gallery of the breed's finest specimens through the years.

The publishers are deeply indebted to those who so graciously provided pictures and information for their outstanding examples of the breed, and earnestly hope that the knowledge presented herein will provide many hours of pleasure to Chihuahua owners.

ELSWORTH HOWELL

Mrs. C. L. Mundey
and her Chihuahuas
Mexico City, Mexico

Natives of Mexico with Chihuahua belonging to Major Mundey

The Lore of the Chihuahua

THE smallest of all breeds of dogs, the Chihuahua is certainly one of the most interesting and most charming. It is not unusual for fanciers of sporting dogs and the larger breeds to express a kind of mild contempt for the tiny breed, but people who disparage the Chihuahua simply do not know the breed.

The breed is intensely loyal to its master, a truly one man dog. While handling by numerous persons may bring a Chihuahua to the point of toleration of all and sundry, its instinct makes for its attachment to a single individual, whom it protects against all comers to the very extent of its powers. Of course, those powers are not great; the dog is too small to accomplish much damage or to serve as a great protection. However, it is surprising how much fury can be contained in the Chihuahua. He resents with all his might, what there is of that might, any molestation of the person he loves and seeks to shield from harm.

There is no need to pamper the Chihuahua, although most owners coddle him beyond reason and good sense. And the Chihuahua likes it all. He is deemed to be somewhat more than a dog, a personality in dog's guise. Especially in Mexico, where dogs are usually ill-treated and ignored, is the Chihuahua accepted as a favored member of the family and so treated. He loves his silken cushions and to be carried about on them, although he is perfectly able to navigate under his own power. He adores to sleep in the bed of his owner, and oftener than not finds some means to ingratiate himself between the sheets. He dotes on the choicest tidbits of food, and is usually to be found in the dining room, cavorting and begging while his owner eats his meal. It is impossible to deny this minute personage.

Quite aside from the presence or absence of hair, the Chihuahua is separate and distinct and not to be confused with the breed known as the Mexican Hairless. They are as unlike in type as they are in size. The Hairless is thought not to be a truly Mexican variety at all. He differs little, if at all, from the Chinese Crested Dog, which is believed to have accompanied invaders across the Bering Strait.

There is some doubt expressed by a few breeders of Chihuahuas that the long coat is a true member of the breed; that it is the result of a cross with the Pomeranian when first introduced into this country. However, the Chihuahua Club of America and The American Kennel Club maintain that the long coated Chihuahua is an authentic division of the breed and that some of the first imports were long coats, particularly Caranza, foundation stud of the famous Meron strain. One well-established strain of long coats, the Don Sergio, has produced some of the finest tiny type Chihuahuas ever shown, all with the exclusive ruby or jeweled eye and with large erect ears, domed heads, and all of the other true Chihuahua features.

Two distinct types of Chihuahuas are shown and raised today, one as popular as the other; namely the cobby type and the deer type. Most breeders prefer the 2½ to 3½ pound cobby male for show and stud, while the deer type bitch of 4 to 5 pounds is preferred for the ideal matron. Although 6 pounds is the maximum specified weight, many truly good bitches have exceeded that weight and proven veritable gold mines to their owners. Ida H. Garrett, well known to all Chihuahua fanciers as one of the oldest and

A blue and white Chinese Crested Dog, owned by
Mr. and Mrs. E. F. Schroerluke of California.

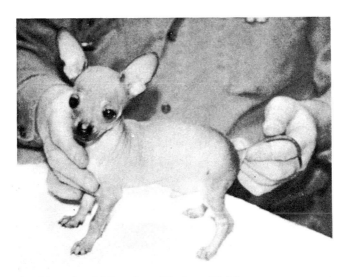

An 11-weeks-old tiny type Mexican Hairless puppy, owned
by Mr. and Mrs. Don Scott of New Mexico.

best authorities on the breed, offered a fabulous price years ago for a ten pound matron whose puppies were of especial excellence, and could not buy the bitch at any price. Today, many a novice writes the breeder for a two pound bitch to breed, little realizing that such procedure is merely courting trouble. A bitch of four pounds is plenty small to breed, and some of the finest tiny puppies come from larger matrons.

Crossing the Toy Manchester and the Amertoy with the Chihuahua is never done by reliable breeders, but there are traces of such crosses in some of our stock today, and perhaps the long muzzle and wedge-shaped head is a throwback to some of those early crosses which were used to breed stamina into early Chihuahuas. For many generations now, only purebreds (to the best of our knowledge) have been used and the true Chihuahua type according to the present accepted Standard has emerged from the scientific crosses within the breed that have been carefully studied. When an occasional "cull" appears in a litter, it should be given away or destroyed, never registered and never used in breeding. This process of careful elimination alone will eventually purify the breed beyond all question.

It is entirely likely that the Chihuahua was originally a small dog, but perhaps larger than those we consider to be correct in type today. The minute size is a matter of selection, and reversion to large size may still occur. Though the Mexican calls such large-sized dogs "degenerados" there is nothing degenerate about them. They are frequently more sound and as typical (except in size) as the best of the smaller miniatures. Retaining these larger bitches of the best type for matrons has already been suggested.

The smallest Chihuahua known by the writer to have matured at close to the minimum weight of one pound, tipped the scales at one pound three ounces at eight months of age. Other "teenies" have been reported, but the one to two pound Chihuahua is so infrequently found that the Standard should probably be changed to read "two to six pounds" instead of "one to six". Chihuahuas generally average four pounds in weight—and even this is a VERY small dog! Much better a sound dog of two, three, or four pounds, than a freak of one pound that is unable to navigate adequately under its own power, and must be carried about on a pillow.

The only breed of dogs truly indigenous to the Western Hemisphere is the Chihuahua. Indeed, even the Chihuahua may have been brought along to America by the prehistoric tribes that invaded America from Asia by way of Bering Strait, but, for all we know to the contrary, the Chihuahua is and has always been American. It is at least as American as the Indian tribes found here by Columbus and the other early explorers.

These Indians had many wolf-like or coyote-like dogs, which were never unified into a specific breed. The coyote is indeed a true dog species and is presumed to be indigenous, but it is feral and no specimen of the breed has ever appeared in a dog show. The close resemblance of the Mexican Hairless Dog to the hairless breeds of China and the Orient, such as the Chinese Crested Dog, leads to the belief that they are a subsequent introduction and are not truly of American origin. Then the Chihuahua is the only breed of domestic dogs which can rightly claim an indigenous American heritage. It is as Mexican as chili con carne.

The Chihuahua has been sadly neglected despite its picturesque, if not too authentic background. Only one book (and the pamphlet by Ida H. Garrett, now out of print) has heretofore been printed on the breed, and few references have been made to it in the magazines of this century. It will be noted, however, that during the past ten or more years, much has been published in dog magazines, and Chihuahua ads now cover several pages in national publications. These facts attest the growing popularity of the breed, even though sources of information about the breed are few, scattered, and, even when gathered together and coordinated, they are of questionable validity. They are a combination of tradition, tall tales, romance, buncombe, surmises, guesses, and old wives' tales. Of authenticated history there is almost none. We are compelled to accept the chaff with the grain and winnow it to come by some small loaf of punitive truth.

The standard authors of dog books either ignore the Chihuahua or dismiss him with a scant three or four para-

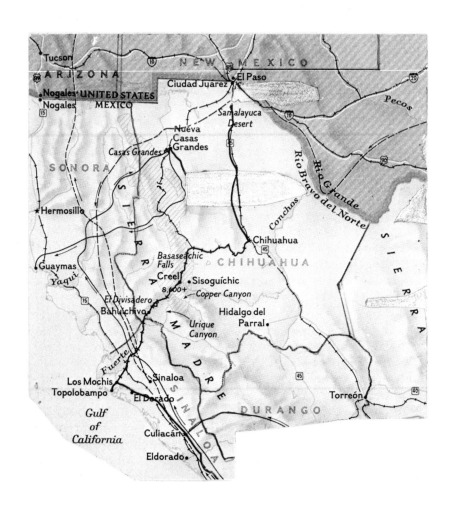

graphs. Those who condescend to mention the breed at all are at variance with one another as to the facts about the breed. They appear not to know and are reluctant to acknowledge their ignorance.

Even James Watson ignores the Chihuahua in his monumental work entitled *The Dog Book,* published in 1905. Watson knew about the breed prior to that time and had considerable experience with it, however. And in "Country Life in America" for the year 1914, he devotes considerable space to the breed in an article which we shall draw upon later.

It is amazing that Ash in his two volume *Dogs and their History* should ignore the Chihuahua entirely. Marples in *Show Dogs* doesn't mention the breed. Count Henri De Bylandt, in his vast treatise in four languages *Dogs of All Nations,* includes a Standard for the Chihuahua, apparently written by somebody who never saw one, including a recommendation for lop ears and loose elbows, otherwise omitting all the essential features of the breed. A single tiny illustration shows a dog with drop ears and, if you please, loose shoulders. The tail in the Standard according to Count De Bylandt, is, God save the mark, docked. The weight is cited to be "about five pounds." In other words, the Standard is worse than merely useless; it is all wrong.

Other writers are equally evasive, not to say ignorant, upon the subject.

Chihuahua is probably a misnomer for the breed, which in its origin belongs more nearly to the southern part of Mexico or to the whole of Mexico than to the State of Chihuahua. That State is a vast domain in itself. It is the largest of the Mexican States, lying just across the Rio Grande River from the western part of Texas.

The State of Chihuahua is a vast elevated valley between two ranges of high mountains. It even yet contains but three sizeable cities, Chihuahua, its capital, Torreon, an industrial center, and Juarez, its port of entry immediately across the Rio Grande from El Paso, Texas.

For the most part, the State of Chihuahua is a vast desert. It is not at all likely that in such an environment a breed of dogs could have been developed and standardized. Just why the difficult name, which even yet is so frequently mispronounced, should have been wished upon a miniature breed of dogs, is to put it mildly, obscure.

Incidentally the correct pronunciation of the word Chihuahua is Chi-WAH-wah, with the accent on the second syllable.

There is a story out of Mexico that the Chihuahua is not a member of the dog species at all, that it is a somewhat dog-like animal first found in the mountains of Chihuahua in a feral state. That pipe dream is on the face of it preposterous. The Chihuahua has all the attributes of a dog, it is fertile when crossed with other breeds of dogs, and in fact it is a dog. All scientific taxonomists include it in the canine species.

A variant of that theory is that the Chihuahua is a cross between a dog and a chipmunk, that the little beast was discovered in the same Chihuahua mountains, that the reason for the breed's long, tough toenails is to enable it the better to climb trees, that it was captured and domesticated, and that the reason for the neglect of the breed by dog fanciers is that it is not a true dog. This cock and bull story requires to be disproved. The Chihuahua is fertile when crossed with other breeds of dogs, and is believed to be infertile when crossed with the chipmunk. Moreover, tree climbing has nothing to do with the requirement for long, tough nails, for the breed is no more arboreal in its habits than is any other breed of dogs.

The third story in the series in the effort to justify the breed's name is that the Chihuahua is a true dog, first found wild in the mountains of Chihuahua. Is it possible to imagine a wild Chihuahua? Think of this delicate little creature trying to fend for itself and to forage for itself in the immense forests of the rugged Sierra Madre Mountains of Chihuahua. The feral species is, in the story, presumed to have become extinct in the latter half of the nineteenth century. The fact is, and we can state it as a fact, that no such species even existed. The Chihuahua is too small and delicate to support itself in a wild state.

THE NORTH AMERICAN DOG
(about the size of a Spaniel)
From Wild Dogs by Col. Hamilton Smith (1843)

THE YOUNG ALCO BROUGHT FROM MEXICO (left)
THE CARRIER DOG OF THE INDIANS (right)
From Wild Dogs by Col. Hamilton Smith (1843)

MISS ROSINA V. CASSELLI
and her troupe of trained Chihuahuas

However, it is only fair that we shall quote from an article published in the British publication "Our Dogs" for August 6, 1904, written by one Miss Rosina V. Casselli, who had a performing troupe of Chihuahuas which were exhibited in British music halls. Miss Casselli appeared to take stock in the theory that the Chihuahua was a wild dog of the Chihuahua mountains. Consideration must be given to the date of publication of the article and to the changes that have occurred in the more than fifty years since it was written. We now know that many of the allegations in the article are mistaken. The breed has been taken up by dog fanciers and the difficulties have been overcome.

MISS ROSINA V. CASSELLI
on
THE CHIHUAHUA DOG

(From "Our Dogs," August 6, 1904)

"REGARDING the Chihuahua dogs, I am in a position to be well posted. Of all the canine breeds there is probably none so little known or understood as the little Chihuahua dogs of Mexico, and which were in their natural state a distinctly Mexican race of wild dogs, very shy, and for their size very savage.

"They inhabit only a limited section of the mountainous state of Chihuahua, from which the dogs derive their name. It is believed that these wild dogs are now extinct, although they are reported by the natives to have been seen up to about fifteen years ago, and it is barely possible that they might still be found in some undisturbed spot.

"These dogs were noted, not only for their extreme smallness, but other peculiarities which they possess.

"Their legs were very slender, and their toenails very long and strong, and very serviceable to them in making their homes, as they lived in holes in the ground. Apart from their size, their most striking feature was their head, which was very round, and from which projected a very short and pointed nose and large standing ears; there was also a peculiar skull formation, found only in this race. In colour they varied somewhat in shade, it was a thorough mixture of reddish black and fawn, in which both vary considerably in different specimens. The hair was short, fine, and thick, and the wild dogs, even when taken young, could

21

not be domesticated, neither would they live any great length of time in captivity.

"The Indians, however, had a way of taking these dogs and crossing them with the small specimens of the domesticated Indian dog, and in this manner produce a domesticated Chihuahua dog, which was kept replenished from the wild stock as much as possible. Although the type was to a certain extent modified and varied, the finer specimens retain it in a most prominent way. Until the opening up of the Mexican Central Railroad, in about the year 1887, and which passes through the section in which the wild dogs were most plentiful, there were plenty of fine specimens to be had, as prior to this time this section was difficult to reach, being in a wild country, hundreds of miles from so-called civilization. The completion of the road, however, brought hordes of tourists and others, who rapidly thinned out the dogs and scattered them in all directions, with the final result that today it is a piece of good luck to secure a really fine specimen.

"Although the wild stock is no longer available, the type is so fixed that very fine specimens still crop up here and there, but there is no certainty when or where such a one can be found, as the natives, although they reaped a rich harvest for a time, failed to provide for the future, as they, with their experience, might have done. I have often been asked why it was that the breed has not been taken in hand by fancy dog breeders. My answers to this is that it was not for want of effort or interest, but failure to get genuine specimens the real cause. There are many difficulties in the way. In the first place they are very difficult to breed, and a thorough understanding of these dogs in particular must be had. Without experience of them, breeding is a most difficult matter, as the chances are all on the side that the mother would die in giving birth to her litter, and even if she survived the ordeal, she is likely to destroy her young, and for a time precaution must be used to prevent this.

"Again, the Chihuahua dogs are very exclusive in their affections, and as a rule will choose a favorite among those

22

that care for them, and become extremely attached, and once such an attachment is formed it is very difficult to break off, and to turn them over to strangers is apt to be a fatal process. When procured at a proper age they are apt to be made a great deal of and spoiled, for they are very affectionate, and demand all sorts of attention. If they don't get it they will pout and mope around for hours and seem to try to make their bodily suffering equal to their mental by hiding in the coldest and draughtiest spots they can find. Neglect of attention soon tells on them, and it is that more than anything else that has produced the very general idea that these dogs can't exist out of their native climate. Such, however is not the case, as they can stand any climate and are strongly constituted. I have never known one to have distemper. Both of my Brazilian dogs had it, I lost one, and just got the other through by a miracle.

"The Chihuahua dogs slept in the small box with these nearly three weeks before we knew what was the matter and not one of them got a touch of it. No one should acquire a Chihuahua dog unless inclined to pander to their whims and notions, and intend to continue to do so. Dog trainers are almost united in their belief that small dogs are useless as performing dogs, but those who have seen my troupe perform must of necessity alter their opinion and admit that the Chihuahua dogs are marvels of intelligence."

A much more likely story of the origin of the Chihuahua breed is that it was derived from a prior breed known as the Techichi, which the Toltecs of the seventh century took over from the yet earlier culture of the Mayans. At least the archeological excavations at Chichen Itza in the Mexican State of Yucatan, point to the Mayans' possession of such a dog.

The Techichi is presumed to have been a long haired, heavy boned, mute dog, none of which attributes pertain to the Chihuahua. Just where the word Techichi came from

23

Mounted Chihuahua, National Museum, Mexico City

Mounted specimens of Chihuahua in the National Museum,
Mexico City

or exactly what it meant is unknown. It may simply have meant dog, for all we know. It is equally obscure just why the Chihuahua should be presumed to derive from a dog of such a description. The evidence attaching the Chihuahua to Mayan culture is very scant.

We know only a little more about the Toltecs than the Mayans. It is rather firmly established that the Toltecs had such a dog as the Techichi and even that the Chihuahua was in process of development during the dominance of that tribe in Mexico. The Monastery of Huejotzingo, on the road leading from the City of Mexico to Puebla, is built in part from materials taken from the Pyramids of Cholula by the Franciscan friars in the first half of the sixteenth century. The pyramids of Cholula are of Toltec construction. In the stones of which the monastery is constructed, are some carvings which represent dogs, presumably the Techichi, and at least two, one a head study and the other picturing a whole dog, that bear a close resemblance to the Chihuahua of the present time.

The Toltecs were abundant at and around Tula, not far from the present capital of Mexico, and in Tula are to be found the most numerous remnants of the Toltec culture. In that area have been found other evidences of the tribe's possession of the Techichi, even if none of the Chihuahua itself.

The Aztecs came from the North and conquered the high plateau of Mexico in the eleventh century and continued to rule it until the arrival of Cortez in the early sixteenth century. There exist rather definite proofs that the Aztecs possessed a minute breed of dogs. This, it appears probable, was the true Chihuahua more or less as we know it today.

However, Prescott in his elaborate and detailed description of the culture and customs of the Aztecs, as he sets it forth in "The Conquest of Mexico" makes no mention whatever of the dogs, which appear to be unworthy of his attention. He describes minutely the Aztecs zoological collection, describes the collection of birds and serpents, but says not a word about their dogs.

The tradition, handed down from generation to generation, still persists in Mexico with a good deal of detail about the dogs the Spaniards found there when they arrived to conquer the country. The tales vary somewhat with their tellers and are therefore not all entirely reliable.

It appears that the Aztecs possessed a minute race of dogs, at least similar to if not identical with the dog we call the Chihuahua. Their ownership was restricted to the royalty and the nobility. Whether their laws forbade the common people to own such dogs or whether the cost and maintenance of such dogs was beyond the means of the commoner is unknown. However, it is known that in practice only the nobles had them.

There is evidence that these small dogs had some obscure religious significance, especially those of certain colors and particularly the blue or bluish gray ones. Killed upon the death of their owners, they were presumed to guide the dead through a labyrinth underworld.

The culture of the Aztecs was marked by an ever increasing luxury for the nobles and for royalty, accompanied with a growing squalor and exploitation of the lower classes and the slaves. The decadence and degeneration that resulted to the nobility from its depraved indulgence and to the slaves from their mistreatment and deprivations contributed to the ease with which Cortez and his handful of soldiers conquered a rich and populous country. Notwithstanding, it is difficult to credit some of the traditions that pertain to the keeping of the tiny dogs which we presume to be identical with the Chihuahua as we know it today.

Included in these tales is one to the effect that one princess possessed a kennel (if we can call a palace a kennel) that housed fifteen hundred little dogs, and that it was not unusual for a lesser noble to possess five hundred small dogs. Each dog was presumed to be attended by a slave whose sole duty was to care for, amuse and entertain his charge. At the death of the dog, his particular slave was killed and buried with him.

These pampered dogs were fed on the minced testicles of virgin slave boys, who were fed a special diet of pungent

26

herbs for three months (or moons) before their mutilation to flavor their flesh that it might tempt the Chihuahua's appetite. This is quite too much for belief, however. It is impossible to gainsay that human testicles may have been fed to the dogs, but that castratos should have been produced in such numbers and for such a purpose, beggars our credulity.

A variant of the story is that the dogs were fed on the flesh of human infants. While it excites our dubiety, it is not beyond possibility. It is a historical fact that the Aztecs fed on human flesh, and Prescott records that the first course of the hundred course dinner of Montezuma, the last of the Aztec monarchs, was a stew or goulash made from the flesh of young boys (*mouchachos de poco edad,* to quote the source of Prescott's statement). It is not beyond the realm of possibility that the leavings from the tables of the king and of the notables should have been fed to the Chihuahuas.

There appears no doubt that the higher classes among the Aztecs maintained their dogs in a degenerative luxury at which our humane instincts and common sense revolt. The Aztec culture in Mexico lasted something like five hundred years and there was time in that half a millennium for a change and evolution of its customs. The sybaritic luxury and degradation of the Aztecs reached its zenith just prior to the arrival of the Spaniards, and if this preposterous care was lavished upon small dogs, as it is alleged, it was probably for only a brief period just prior to the conquest. It is entirely likely that these tales have been much exaggerated as they have been handed down by word of mouth through the generations since the events occurred. The kennels of fifteen hundred dogs might, if truth were known, dwindle to fifty. Instead of feeding the dogs the flesh of children, it may be that they were fed the same food that the children ate. Instead of one slave to each dog, the truth may be that slaves were employed as caretakers for the dogs. It is impossible to accept too seriously unconfirmed traditions that may have been exaggerated with every re-telling through the generations. On the other hand, they may be true, and without doubt had some points of departure in fact.

All Aztec wealth was confiscated by Cortez and his Spanish crew of cut-throats; the culture of the tribe was disrupted and much of it lost. Henceforth, we are to know little about the Chihuahua until the nineteenth century.

There is alleged to be extant a letter or report written by Christopher Columbus to the King of Spain in which he declares that he found in Cuba "a small kind of dogs, which were mute and did not bark, as usual, but were domesticated." Whether these dogs may have been Chihuahuas or Techichi, we have no way of knowing. Cuba is but a short distance from Mexico and there was doubtless some intercourse between that island and the mainland.

Papillon, Ch. Cadaga's Kerry.

There appears little doubt that the breed of dogs we now call the Papillon has descended from a tiny dog brought back from the New World by sailors in the second voyage of Columbus or by others of the Spanish conquistadores. The Papillon, despite the differences that are bound to arise in a breed in the course of so many centuries, bears an unmistakable resemblance to the Chihuahua, especially in the carriage of its ears. There is no intimation that there have not been infusions of the blood of other breeds in the making of the Papillon; it is doubtless not a pure descendant of the Chihuahua. However, the very existence

28

of such a breed as the Papillon and the assurance of its descent from minute dogs which the Spaniards had found in the Caribbean colonies is the best proof we possess that the natives possessed the Chihuahua, perhaps not exactly as we know it today, but a dog of similar size and structure. The name by which this breed was called by the Aztecs we have no way of knowing. It would probably be historically more sound to name it the Azteca than the Chihuahua.

The first of these dogs of which we have historical data were discovered in 1850 near Casas Grandes, Chihuahua, in some ruins said to be those of a palace built by Montezuma I. However, it is to be doubted that the Aztec emperors were enough interested in Chihuahua to build a palace in a province so remote, inaccessible, and sparsely inhabited. The ruin was probably that of a Spanish or Mexican hacienda, fallen into disrepair and abandoned. The dogs, when found, were in the possession of some ignorant peons, who were glad to part with them for a few pesos. They are said to have had long nails, the molera, and the spreading ears of the modern Chihuahua, which marks them as authentic members of the breed, even if not good ones. Shortly thereafter other specimens were turned up in other parts of Mexico. This was in the era shortly after the war between the United States and Mexico. Prior to the American invasion, little interest was shown or cognizance taken of canine species or varieties, and it is to be wondered at that the Chihuahua breed should have retained its purity without intermixture through its many years in the hands of ignorant, careless, and stupid peons. It is to be suspected that the breed was so small as to make difficult the mating with larger dogs, which must have gone far toward preserving its integrity.

So little is known about the small dogs which General Santa Ana had in his camp before the Battle of San Jacinto that it is impossible to claim them definitely. Santa Ana was a dope-crazed dictator of Mexico, a veritable Hitler in his power and ruthlessness. He was picked up, disguised as a peon, by the American forces after the Battle of San Jacinto, abandoning his dogs, about which nothing since

29

has been learned. It is established that they were very small and of a brownish color, and that before they were abandoned in the battle, Santa Ana was meticulous about their care and comfort in the campaign.

In the late nineteenth century it was commonplace for peons to peddle Chihuahuas to tourists at Juarez, across the river from El Paso, Texas. Most of the Chihuahuas were unsound and their chief attraction for buyers was in their size, or lack of size. Their cost was so small that most buyers failed to appreciate them and most of such dogs soon died of cold and neglect. Where the vendors obtained their supply of such dogs, which was constant, is difficult to surmise. The sums for which they were sold were inadequate to justify their breeding and rearing, even considering the low prices of the time and the rate of exchange between American and Mexican currencies.

The only one of such transactions of which we have an authentic record is that recorded by James Watson in an article published in 1914 in "Country Life in America." Watson was a famous expert judge of dogs, and his *The Dog Book* is a standard work upon the subject. As we have noted before, he did not include the Chihuahua in the breeds he discussed in it.

The Country Life article is so interesting and throws so much light upon the subject that it is worth quoting from *in extenso*:

"THE CHIHUAHUA DOG"

By James Watson

(from Country Life In America, March, 1914)

"Now that the Newfoundland seems to be practically extinct as a show dog and the Boston Terrier cannot be claimed to be indigenous, the only truly North American dog appears to be the Chihuahua of Mexico. There is no dog exactly like it to be found anywhere else, so that there can be no claim made as to its being from elsewhere. As a matter of fact, the small dogs we see at our shows classified as Chihuahuas are exceptionally rare and come, one might almost say, by chance. Perhaps not altogether that, but there is no definite type sought for, and you see different looking puppies in the litters, one of which may be very small, and it is these small ones that our exhibitors seek for.

"The kind I prefer is the smooth, white or fawn, dog. The ears are somewhat large, held erect, not after the manner of the Pomeranian or French Bulldog, but flaring to one side. There is also a peculiarity as to the tail. It is long for the size of the dog, and my preference is for its being carried hoop fashion over the middle of the back, the point of the tail almost touching the root. The Foxhound comes the nearest to this tail carriage, but if a Hound made a full circle, the shortness of his tail would make the loop ridiculously small for the size of the dog, whereas the extra length of the Chihuahua's tail avoids this suggestion and the hoop sets off the dog to perfection.

"I have noticed the neglect on the part of some owners as to the toenails. In Mexico, where they trot about on the dirt floors and about the 'dobe, the nails are kept worn down, but as pets with us the nails grow faster than they wear, soon become claws and split the toes apart, flatten them out and twist them to one side. The nails should be trimmed, which can be easily done with scissors or with a sharp pen knife.

"My connection with the Chihuahua began in the spring of 1888, when I made my first judging trip to the Coast. I had stopped off at El Paso so as to cross the river and say I had been in Mexico. As I was awaiting the arrival of the train for the West, I saw a Mexican standing with a very small dog in his hand. I knew enough Spanish to ask him 'How much?' He replied $5, and as I was pulling out the money another man rushed up and advised me that he could speak English, so I amusedly said, 'Ask him if he will take $4.' After a most animated conversation I was advised that he would take $3. That purchase rankled on my conscience for many years, and not until I had confided in a doggy Father of the church and he said I was justified in paying the $3, did the matter settle in my mind. I have never seen another like this little Manzanita, as she was named. Had it not been that we had no Pomeranians in the country at the time I should have said she was of that kin. Her coat was like beaver fur both as to color and texture, and she was so small that I carried her in my coat pocket till I got to Los Angeles, and there got the smallest size chip basket, in which she had plenty of room. A boy at the San Francisco show exclaimed at sight of her, 'Oh, an Arizona dog,' and a gentleman in Germantown stopped me one day and said he had not seen one of those dogs since he had been in Arizona a few years ago. When Manzanita died of pneumonia the following winter I tried all manner of ways to get some information from Arizonians, as I wanted another. It was not until my fourth trip to the Coast that I had an opportunity to take a Southern route, and I chose the Santa Fe, as the boy in the show had said something about Indians having these dogs, and I could easily reach one or two reservations from Gallup and elsewhere. There was no result, and the advice got there was that it was the southern side of the state along the Mexican border I had to go and stop off here and there.

"Homeward bound I took that advice and stopped off at Tucson, where I got a very nice black-and-tan dog, but all the others were larger than I wanted, so I moved on to El Paso and spent three days there, where I proceeded to pick up half a dozen as small as I could get them and illustrating what seemed to be distinctions in type. Some ran to the Terrier type, others to a longer body and shorter legs, these being all red and pretty well coated. I got one of each of these, the Terrier type one, named Juarez Belle, easily becoming a champion. She was pure white and beautifully built, having perfect feet and forelegs, as also had the Tucson dog. I then got a litter of three, all black and white and all varying in coat, a smooth, a furry one, and one with a Maltese coat. I wound up by picking a liver-and-white out of another litter, a very small dog. I had had bad luck with all but the red and white, the others succumbing in the winter.

"Last year on my way home from Santa Rosa I spent two

32

days at El Paso and Juarez and finally succeeded in getting what I hold was the best of the breed I have ever seen—a small smooth-coated dog, seven months old, and weighing short of sixteen ounces on the drug store scales, all white except for a black spot at the root of the tail. That dog I unfortunately lost in Philadelphia when carrying it about in a small basket and paying some business calls. I put it down somewhere, and that was the last of my best Chihuahua.

"The Chihuahua seems to be gaining slightly, as at the Islip show there were five, and that without Mr. McGovern's pair which had been to so many shows. They are bright and smart little dogs, very affectionate, and they have the great advantage of a short coat, which can be readily kept clean by brushing and an occasional washing. Another point about short coated dogs is that they never get 'out of coat' as longer coated breeds do, and then look all wrong.

"There is just one trouble and that is getting them acclimated and capable of standing our winter. With the exception of my first buy, made in April, all I subsequently got were October purchases. If it had not been for the disturbances about Juarez I would have gone there last June to look up some more, but the advice I got was to stay at home till things were more settled.

"As I have said, these little house dogs are of all shapes, varying as to size, and of many colors. As to these points the Mexican cares little. His one indication of the purity of the breeding is the orifice in the centre of the skull— the great peculiarity of this breed and found in no other."

It is necessary to remind the reader of the date of Mr. Watson's article and to emphasize his authority in the world of dogs. It seems to us now that he was singularly uninformed about the breed, in spite of his extensive experience with it and intense interest in it. Since he wrote, a definite concept of the breed has been formulated and accepted and uniformity has developed; the Chihuahua Club of America has been formed; a Standard of excellence has been formulated and revised; the breed has ceased to be a rare one; grossly oversized dogs have largely disappeared; the difficulties of acclimatization have been overcome, since the largest part of the best Chihuahuas are bred and reared in the United States itself.

The Terrier type of dog which Watson admired, and one of which he piloted to a championship, no longer is tolerated in the show ring, and the looped tail on the Chihuahua would be considered as ridiculous as Watson conceived that such a tail would be on a Foxhound.

The article is reprinted here, not for the purpose of explaining to the reader what the Chihuahua of the present time should be like, but rather to give him some ideas of the false concepts about the breed entertained—and that by a foremost authority—in the early years of this century.

Further light is shed on the Chihuahua Watson bought in Chihuahua by an article signed "J.W." in "The American Kennel Register" for May 1888. The identity of J. W. as James Watson is unquestioned, since he refers in the article to his judging of the San Francisco dog show and since it is known that Watson judged the classes of non-sporting dogs at the show of the Pacific Kennel Club on April 4, 5, 6, and 7, 1888. After some discussion of some rough Mexican Terriers, which he disparagingly describes, he says:

"I tried my best to get hold of a decent animal of the toy type, but failed at Paso del Norte; however, just as I was waiting for the train at El Paso I came across a Mexican on the platform who had the cutest little puppy I ever saw. A red Terrier, flesh-colored nose, Pug tail, but not twisted, and a thick soft coat shooting out strongly. It had the hole of the Chihuahua dog in the skull, and with very little trouble we exchanged dollars and dog. I carried it without any trouble in my pocket for two days and after that in the smallest size lunch basket for two weeks, during which it did the Yosemite trip and proved to be the best introduction I could get on my travels. The Mexican said it was four months old, but I am sure he overstated the age, so as to make it appear an extremely small one, nevertheless it was one of the best behaved puppies I ever possessed or heard of, and never once during our four weeks' journey in company did she fail to notify me that it was necessary for her to be let out of her basket, which at Sacramento was exchanged for a larger size. At other times there was neither bark nor whimper, and not one of the long-eared, lynx-eyed, quarter-cent-a-mile fiends on the railroads ever detected her presence. We landed safely in Philadelphia and the puppy was duly named Manzanita in view of her standing the four weeks' journey. The manzanita is a shrub met with on the Sierras which in addition to its gray foliage and light red bark is remarkable for its toughness. Although this was the only specimen of the soft coated kind I came across they must be well known in Mexico, for a San Francisco boy who had been in the country at once recognized her as a "Mexican dog." A gentleman in Germantown also asked me how my "Mexican dog" was getting along, he having recognized her breed when seeing her on the street one day. Surely some of the Register readers can give particulars respecting these Mexican breeds, probably the only North American breeds outside the Esquimaux.

" * * * I have simply described what I saw, nothing more, nothing less, and to summarize the result of my observations I would say, there are in Mexico certain distinct types of Terriers and toys, other than the hairless dog, of which specimens are often seen in the States, but that nowhere in the United States is there anything that has not been imported within recent years. * * *

"I should like very much to hear from some of my readers with regard to the dogs of Mexico, as I was greatly taken up with them."

(signed) "J.W."

The first Chihuahua exhibited in America was Chi Chigas, entered by William H. McCracken in the show of the Philadelphia Kennel Club, which was held September 16, 17, 18, and 19, 1884. This dog was entered as a "Chihuahua Terrier" in the class for Miscellaneous or Foreign dogs, and was placed last in his class with a V.H.C. (very highly commended). The position in the list of awards has no significance whatever, since no judge of that day was prepared to judge Chihuahuas intelligently. Even in the Watson article it is apparent that Watson, himself, who was one of the most scholarly and expert judges of the period, in 1887 had no adequate concept about the requirements of the breed.

The first Chihuahua to become a champion of record under the rules of The American Kennel Club was Champion Beppie, 85,317, the property of Mrs. L. A. McLean of Hackensack, New Jersey. Beppie was white and fawn, by Bonito out of Carlotta, was whelped February 2, 1903, and was registered in 1905. However, a championship at that time did not mean what it does today. The championship rating of a show was based upon the entire number of dogs of all breeds entered in it and not upon the numbers of the respective breeds, as at present. The winner of the winners class, whether there was one dog or a hundred dogs in the competition, received the same championship rating as the most numerous breed in the show. Thus it was possible for a dog to become a champion without meeting, not to mention defeating, any other dog of his breed or of any breed. For such breeds as the Chihuahua in its early days, championship was a somewhat empty honor.

The first registration of a Chihuahua in the American Kennel Club Studbook was of Midget, 82,291, registered by H. Raynor of El Paso, Texas. The dog was whelped July 18, 1903, bred by its owner, and entered in the Studbook of 1904. He was by Pluto out of Blanca, neither of which was registered, as would now be required, although their pedigrees were stated. In the same number of the Stud-book was registered Bonito, 2,292, a litter sister to Midget. Of the five entries in that year, four were registered by the same H. Raynor, and the fifth was bred by Mr. Raynor and registered in the name of J. M. Lee of Los Angeles.

In that year of 1904, only eleven Chihuahuas were ex-hibited in the entire United States, mostly in Miscellaneous classes. By 1916, the number of Chihuahuas exhibited in the entire country had climbed only to fifty.

But the unique, attractive qualities of the Chihuahua were bound to catch the interest of the dog fancy. The Chihuahua Club of America was organized in 1923 and became a mem-ber of the American Kennel Club. Its activities have given an impetus to the breed that has zoomed it to high place in the Top Ten of all breeds in registrations each year.

By 1967, registrations had climbed to over 37,000 for the year, and the Chihuahua ranked fifth of all breeds, exceeded only by Poodles, German Shepherd Dogs, Beagles and Dach-shunds. In 1968 registrations dropped off somewhat to a 33,000 level, and the Miniature Schnauzer took over fifth place. In 1970, there were 28,833 Chihuahuas registered dur-ing the year, and the breed was being pressed for its sixth place in the rankings by a dog of opposite extreme, the Saint Bernard.

The rise of the Chihuahua in England has been similarly impressive. Although individual Chihuahuas had been im-ported to Britain as long ago as 1930, it was not until 1954 that Crufts awarded Challenge Certificates for the breed. In 1952, there were no Chihuahuas registered with the English Kennel Club. In 1969, however, 4,149 (2,714 Smooths and 1,435 Long Coats) were registered—making it second only to the Yorkshire Terrier of all Toy breeds, and the 13th highest total of all breeds. Quality has improved apace.

The standard of perfection for the breed, compiled and adopted by the Chihuahua Club of America in 1923, has been revised (with approval of the American Kennel Club) twice—on August 14, 1934 and on January 12, 1954. This latest revision is presented on Page 87 of this book.

The Chihuahua Club of America initiated a separately held Specialty Show, limited to Chihuahuas only, in 1946. It attracted an entry of 71 for the famous all-rounder judge, Mr. Forest N. Hall of Dallas, Texas. Mr. Hall is much interested in Mexican show activities and has judged there often, and his native Texas still harbors more Chihuahuas than any other State, probably because of its proximity to Mexico.

Mexican dogs, for the most part, are not so scientifically bred nor reared as those in the United States. There are exceptions to that statement, however.

The Chihuahua was long accounted to be delicate and unhealthy, which was in fact true of many of the early importations. Bred without discrimination and reared without knowledge of feeding and sanitation, deliberately starved for the purpose of keeping them small, they were puny and unsound. Nor was much regard paid to type. Anything that was small enough and was a dog was salable as a Chihuahua.

The facts are that the Chihuahua, given half a chance, is one of the most vigorous and disease-resistant of all dogs. Size is still a desideratum, but under the aegis of the Chihuahua Club of America, concessions in the matter of size are made to type and soundness. No longer in the shows does a dog win on size alone. He has to be both typical and sound. Of course he must be small, but cripples, however small, receive short shrift at the hands of the judges.

Van der Meid photo

CH. RAYAL'S SUSANITA with her son and daughter, Lillibet and Angus. They were sired by Ch. Rayal's Prince Lucky. Owned and bred by Alberta E. Booth.

Mrs. Henrietta Proctor Donnell, with some of her Etty Haven
champions of the 1920s.

Early Chihuahuas

FAMOUS SIRES AND DAMS, AND BLOODLINE BEGINNINGS

By Rev. Russell E. Kauffman

THE American Kennel Club Studbook published in 1890 is the first to mention the Chihuahua. It recorded the wins of ANNO, first at Detroit, owned by Rose M. Prince; BOB, "equal first," New York, Mrs. F. Siegrist; EYAH, second, Detroit, Mrs. J. Wakefield; PEPITY, first, Detroit, Mrs. Wakefield. These dogs were of course unregistered, and the class in which they were shown was not designated.

1894 records show the wins of two: CHIHUAHUERIA, first, Denver, F. W. Broad; and NITA, first novice, Louisville, H. B. Dunbar. The year 1896 was graced with four entries; 1898 with one; 1899 with four; and 1900 with four. In 1901 fifteen appeared; five were listed in 1902; and nine in 1903. These figures show the slow growth of Chihuahuas as bench show entrants in the very early days.

The first Chihuahua champion was BEPPIE, 85,317, owned and bred by Mrs. L. A. McLean of Hackensack, N. J. Beppie was a fawn and white, whelped February 2, 1903, out of Carlotta by Bonito. Her championship was recorded in the 1908 Studbook. Five dogs and two bitches were registered in that book, including the now famous EL CAPITAN,

116,203, whelped Sept. 25, 1906, owned and bred by H. K. Edwards of Shawnee, Oklahoma, and CHULA, 114,448, whelped Feb. 22, 1903, owned by Mrs. C. D. Atwood and bred by Susana Hernadez. Chula finished for the championship the following year.

This brings us up to the time that was really the beginning of this now popular little tinyette as an established toy breed in the United States and a consistent contender for top honors in our present-day bench shows. In 1916 the number of Chihuahuas exhibited in the entire country totaled only fifty. We cannot fairly estimate the number of dogs then in American homes, for many good Chihuahuas were never registered and never exhibited. But by the end of 1949 the Chihuahua had climbed to eighth place among A.K.C. registered breeds, showing the most phenomenal growth of 73% during the year, with 7,156 registrations, second only to the Peke in the toy group.

With the organization of the Chihuahua Club of America in 1923, standardization became possible and Chihuahua breeding took on a more serious aspect. Much credit must be given Mrs. Ida H. Garrett, Mrs. Charles Dobbs, Charles Stewart, Mrs. L. A. McLean, Mrs. C. D. Atwood, Mrs. Ann Radcliffe, Mrs. Bertha Peaster, and others of the early day fanciers for their perseverance and loyalty to the breed. The untiring efforts of such pioneers have made possible the present-day Chihuahua.

ORIGIN OF MERON AND PERRITO STRAINS

There is authentic evidence that the two outstanding strains of the breed emanated from the same foundation stud, Caranza. Early in the nineteen hundreds Owen Wister, who wrote *The Virginian,* visited Mexico to secure local color for some of his painting. There in some mountainous region he and his friend Charles Stewart, who had accompanied him, saw their first Chihuahuas and purchased Caranza and others for the purpose of breeding them on their estate in Philadelphia. The inferior types were given to Stewart, who lived on the estate. Ida H. Garrett writes: "The Stewarts lived in an ancient interesting house in which were Dutch ovens built into the walls. When I went there to visit Mr. Wister and the Stewarts, I saw the various ovens full of Chihuahua mothers with litters. These ovens were kept at right temperature by a little wood fire laid in the fireplace." Caranza was the "chief" of the Chihuahua family in the Wister home. Mrs. Garrett gives us this detailed description of him: "He was about 2½ or 3 pounds, of a dark fiery red, a LONG HAIRED dog his tail like that of a squirrel. His head was perfect by the Standard we have today. His eyes were ruby red, ears fringed not unlike those of the Papillon. He was a ducky type, shorter on legs than length of back. I think he was the most loving and beautiful creature in dog flesh I ever saw."

Caranza met with a tragic death on the Wister estate, but only after he had started the finest strain of Chihuahuas known in the United States even today. A terrible storm had swept Philadelphia and felled a great oak tree on the Wister estate. Caranza worked his way through the limbs to the trunk of the fallen tree and ran down the trunk toward the upturned roots, looking much like a squirrel to his aging and slightly blind friend, a great Dane, who grabbed Caranza and killed him. The Dane died soon after the tragedy.

As Caranza was the best type and the most active of the Mexican imports he was used more than another stud owned by Mr. Wister—a gray-sable smooth coat of about the same diminutive size. The latter stud was later given to Mr. Stewart and to this day most of the dogs of that strain run to the sable color.

The first Meron that went to a championship was very close coated and of a pale fawn or tan color with creamy under parts of the body. He was owned by Mrs. Ann Radcliffe who got him direct from the Stewarts. Mrs. Radcliffe was the first to register any of the Wister-Stewart dogs. The Wisters were really opposed to registrations, but after Mrs. Radcliffe began to register the dogs, the Wisters and Stewarts exchanged for registered ones and carried on their breeding program with both registered and non-registered stock. No pedigrees backed the first Merons except the

Semi-long Coat "SUGAR"
Don Sergio strain crossed with Meron, La Reina Kennels,
Jacksonville, Florida

AMIGO MIO of LA REINA
Sired by Ch. Don Rubio Grudier
Golden fawn stud owned by La Reina Kennels,
Jacksonville, Florida

names of the Mexican parents of Caranza (ex Deano by Duke).

Mrs. Radcliffe registered the first Little Meron on his wins, and made him a champion. He in turn sired Ch. Little Meron III, bred by Mrs. H. Diehl of San Antonio, Texas, and out of an imported dam, Lady Goldie (ex Dona Mignon by Don Oro). Mrs. Garrett bought Ch. Little Meron III for a price well up in three figures, and made him a champion in three shows, registering him on his 10 point wins. This outstanding Meron was very much like his sire, but better in type, more sturdy, and darker in color. Many outstanding champions are among his grandsons and granddaughters and their progeny. It is believed that the Merons have contributed more Chihuahuas of the best type than all other families of the breed put together.

Mrs. Garrett recalls the Chihuahua Specialty Show in Chicago in 1935, where sixteen champions entered the ring to compete for Best of Breed, and every one a Meron, sons or grandsons of Ch. Little Meron, a four pound Best of Breed winner then near five years of age.

Although there are still a few breeders who refuse to accept the long coated Chihuahua as a purebred, it is an established fact that the Merons throw more long coats than any other strain, and the Meron remains the foundation strain of the breed.

A dam much like the Merons in type, Ch. Lady Vita, was imported by Mrs. Garrett and crossed with her El Capitan, produced some of the best of the early Chihuahuas. This blood, along with the blood of such well-known early champions at Little Perrito, Bugg's Breeze and Garrett's Gengibre was successfully crossed with the early Merons to produce more excellent type.

Though some are of the opinion that the Perrito strain was of imported origin different from the Meron, Mrs. Garrett declares that the famed Caranza was the foundation sire of both strains. We know that the first Perrito was bred to Ch. Sonora (ex Betty II by Donnie II) to produce Ch. Perrito II, the outstanding sire of the line, a tiny not over two pounds in weight, lemon color, who lived but eight years and sired

Mrs. Bertha Peaster of famous La Rex Doll prefix, began breeding and exhibiting Chihuahuas before World War I. The four dogs shown with her in this photograph, weighing between one and one half to three pounds each, are, left to right: Ch. Little Panchor, Ch. Little Conchita, Ch. La Rex Doll Snowdrop and Ch. Peaster's Little Juanita.

Three celebrated champions of La Rex Doll Kennels in the 1920s: La Rex Doll Chiquelo, Juanita Queen, and La Rex Doll Donero.

only twelve litters, each of four puppies. This little champion born in 1920 headed a list of eleven Perritos registered over a period of seven years. Perrito VI sired the famous Ch. Si Si Oro Principe in 1930, possibly the last to be registered by a Perrito sire of direct descent. Perrito 10 and his son El Feljo should both have had their day on the bench, according to Mrs. Garrett, who declared them to be two of the best of their day or the present. Perrito 10 was a three pound salmon with ruby eyes.

LA REX DOLL CHIHUAHUAS

Prominent in the 1920s was the La Rex Doll line of fine Chihuahuas, originating with Mrs. Bertha Peaster of Philadelphia whose first dogs came from the Wister-Stewart kennels in that same city. Sonora, the first Peaster purchase, weighed but three pounds, but mated with Atwood's imported Chiquelo produced five puppies. The bitches were retained as foundation dams of this famous strain. A male out of this litter, Peaster's Little Chiquelo, was bred to Mrs. Alling's Chi Tanta Royal, and produced that grand little sensation at every bench show where he was exhibited, Ch. Peaster's Little Pedro, a solid fawn weighing about a pound and a half. Little Pedro is the sire of many La Rex Doll Chihuahuas, and he and Ch. Little Meron III have probably sired more progeny than any other males of this breed.

Candy Kid, said by Mrs. Garrett to be better than most anything of today, from Mexican import parentage, was crossed with Ch. Peaster's Little Conchita, and produced La Rex Doll Donna Ana, found in many pedigrees today. Mrs. Garrett also says of the La Rex Doll line, "A male called Slim (imported from Mexico by Dr. Speare of the U.S.N.) and crossed into the Meron line was responsible for many of the fine dogs brought out by Mrs. Peaster."

PAUL MOURMAN'S MINIATURA LINE

With a little bitch he called Rosita (Ex Donna Anita by Perrito II), Merons from Garrett stock, and various Chihuahuas from the stock of Narcissa Clewell and Bertha Peaster (most of which had the Meron line in them), this little known musician-breeder originated the Miniatura line of fine Chihuahuas. Mr. Mourman was greatly hampered by poor health and financial reverses but with the aid of Mrs. Garrett and a New Orleans veterinarian cared for his dogs and produced some outstanding sires and dams of the breed, including Ch. Little Pipo of Miniatura and Little Litina of Miniatura.

OTHER WELL-KNOWN STRAINS ARE STARTED

Edith Rhodes' Boo Strain of Chihuahuas in Michigan; the McCord line in California; Mrs. M. E. Hood and her line of Texas Merons and out-crosses in San Antonio; Mayme Cole Holmes with her line of Perraltos in Kansas; the Attas lines in Texas—these and others followed in rapid succession the earlier lines mentioned in preceding paragraphs, all of them from direct descendants and out-crosses of the famous Meron-Perrito Chihuahuas.

LA ORO LINE

Another now famous line appearing about the same time, or in the early 1930's was the La Oro line bred by Anna B. Vinyard. Here was a combination of the Meron, Perrito, Miniatura lines with several imported bitches among which was Alita Beebee, a dam of record. The most famous of the La Oro sires was the diminutive Ch. Si Si Oro Principe who, according to Mrs. Vinyard, holds the all-time record of having sired the greatest number of champion get, with Ch. La Rex Doll Chicuelo second, and Don Apache third.

Si Si was whelped March 20, 1930, out of Aieda A by Perrito VI. He is credited with possessing most of the good qualities of his well-known great-grandsires: Ch. Perrito II, Ch. Villa, Ch. Little Meron, and Ch. Chiquito—names familiar to every Chihuahua breeder from coast to coast. From the Meron strain he inherited his true Chihuahua expression and full, typey head; and from the Perrito, his aggressiveness and unexcelled showmanship.

Perhaps the most notable of the four champion males and the seven champion bitches sired by Si Si, was Ch. Bebita-De-Oro-Gitanilla (gold-baby-of-Gypsy-girl). In 1937 this bitch

48

CH. LA ORO PERRILA, CH. MI ORO DON MERON
and CH. SI SI ORO PRINCIPE
The first three champions of
Mrs. Anna B. Vinyard, Cincinnati, Ohio

CHAMPION SI SI ORO PRINCIPE
Sire: Perrito VI   Dam: Aeida A.
Breeder and owner: Mrs. Anna B. Vinyard

placed second best American-Bred Toy in the United States after only three months of showing. She held the record for winning the largest toy group in Chicago that same year, and also the next six straight groups in which she was shown.

DON RUBIO CHIHUAHUAS

In the later 1930's the Rhodes and Pearson lines of both smooth and long coated Chihuahuas appeared. They have been responsible for many of the good ones on the West Coast. However, the first to go to the Pacific Coast was Sneath's Chiquito, and Mrs. Evelyn Brush started her line of Don Rubio Chihuahuas from that dog. Sneaths sold all they had to Mrs. Brush (now Benner), a totally different line from the Merons. Sneath's Chiquito was out of Bonita V by Chiquito (ex Florenda by Elmoreno). Florenda was a black import from Mexico, and Elmoreno, also imported, was a five pound red seal with a very broad head and short face. Sneath's Chiquito himself was a splashed black, white, and seal with a slender, long body; a wonderful sire.

Ch. Brush's Don Rubio was registered on his many California wins and for many years was known as the Chihuahua that had won more trophies than any ever shown, until the advent of the late Ch. Meronette Grudier. Don Rubio was sired by Juano (ex Teracina by Tommy Tucker) and out of Merilla (ex Salamanda by Bab's Bobo). Rubio was a red fawn of medium size, good head and ears, rather long in legs, and very aggressive. He is the foundation stud of a long line of solid reds, many of which are much more typey than their famous ancestor.

THE DON APACHE LINE OF GRUDIER CHIHUAHUAS

Though one of the most recent of the famous lines of Chihuahuas, the Don Apache strain is well established and has produced many notable winners. Apache himself was far from show type—he was large, six pounds in weight—but he possessed very large, dark, expressive eyes well set in a broad head with unusually large ears. These excellent features he consistently transmitted to his get. The abundant

50

coat, furry tail and well developed ruff are also characteristic of this line of Chihuahuas. Apache is out of Perrita Cherry Blossom and sired by a son of Si Si, Ch. Oro De Lay, a pure Perrito. When crossed with the Meron progeny of Ch. Little Meron IV, exceptionally fine puppies have been produced, including the late Ch. Meronette Grudier whose record of wins has seldom if ever been topped. The names Grudier and Don Apache have come to be synonymous in Chihuahua language.

PERRALTO LINE OF MAYME COLE HOLMES

Top stud in this well-known kennel in Kansas for many years was Perralto, out of Mattalee (ex Maritza by Ch. Chum of Fleurette) and sired by the famous El Feljo (ex Mitta Mira by Ch. Perrito X). Montoyo II and Poncho Villa Cola carry on the Perralto type and characteristics, strong in the best blood of the La Oro lines and outcrosses from genuine Perrito stock of earlier days. Perraltos are known for their fine domed heads, cobby bodies, and diminutive size.

ORIGIN OF LONG COATED LINE OF DON SERGIOS

More than twenty years ago the first Don Sergio was produced by mating Mrs. L. Palmer's fine little apricot stud El Feljo to Quita, by her owner, Sarah Holland of Duxbury, Mass. Sergio was a white long coat with chocolate markings, of about three pounds weight. He had a wonderful head, ruby eyes, large well-fringed erect ears, and a beautiful plumed tail. This dog was acquired by Mr. and Mrs. John T. Kinsman of Chicago and Boca Raton, Florida, when he was about a year old. He had sired a few puppies at that time, but was not used again until six years later. His own puppies were few, but among them were five champion long coats, two of which were outstanding. One, Sela Donna, bred by Mrs. Kinsman's sister, Mrs. McCoy, was a flyer, winning nine straight shows, including the International. The other, Ch. Don Sergio of Boca Raton, won the highest award offered by the Chihuahua Club of America, the trophy for most Best of Breed wins, in 1941.

A South American import, Cheateu, was bought from a native breeder of long coats in Colombia by Louis Weitz of

CH. LUCE'S LITTLE FLASH (Ch. El Juguete's Flash ex Luce's Blue Pansy). A prolific sire and steady winner, he is owned by Mrs. Rozel G. Luce of Kennedy, New York.

CH. LUCE'S FLASH-E-GAYLA, litter sister of Ch. Luce's Little Flash, was Best of Variety at Westminster in 1961. Owner is Mrs. Luce.

Chicago in 1930. The original stock was from Brazil. Cheateu is the great-grand-dam of the Brazilian branch of the Sergio strain, and the only Chihuahua of this blood in the United States, except those of her offspring crossed with Sergio. Cheateu was mated with Don Sergio, producing Donna Anita. She in turn was mated with her sire, producing Brazilian Brown Chiquita, who, bred back to her sire and grandsire, produced the lovely Ch. Brazilian Brown Joy, in 1939. This cross with Brazilian blood greatly strengthened and beautified the strain, which remains the only absolutely pure long coat line of Chihuahuas.

GREAT SIRES AND DAMS (1920 to 1939)
as named by Anna B. Vinyard

Sires: Ch. Little Meron III
Ch. Boo's Mitzi Meron
Ch. La Rex Doll Chicuelo
Ch. Little Pipo of Miniatura
Ch. Imp of Erebus
Ch. Perrito II
Perrito VI
Perrito X
Ch. Suni Reye
Ch. Mi Oro Don Meron
Ch. Bishop's Chiquito
Ch. Rhodes' Tiny Tim
Ch. Don Sergio
Don Apache
Ch. Si Si Oro Principe.

Dams: Ch. Hood's Brownie Dear
Ch. La Rex Doll Ora
Diadem Rose Marie
La Ora Paloma
Aeida A
Little Litina of Miniatura
Ch. La Oro Jaspeada
Ch. Attas' Concha Curcera
Alita Beebee.

CH. HURD'S BABE IN THE WOODS pictured as she scored 1963 BOV over 24 Chihuahuas. Babe is a fine example of the quality Chihuahuas bred by her sire, Ch. Hurd's Tequilla Kid, sire of 14 champions. Ch. Tequilla was the first champion bred by Max and Marie Hurd. The Hurds started in the breed in 1958, and by 1970 had bred and/or owned 36 champions.

CH. HURD'S LIL INDIAN, a 1967 Group winner. Indian is also a daughter of Ch. Hurd's Tequilla Kid. She finished to her championship by going Best of Winners at the 1964 Chihuahua Club of America Specialty. Owned by the Hurds.

Bloodlines and Sires of More Recent Years

By Rev. Russell E. Kauffman

ESTABLISHED bloodlines of yesterday have perhaps been somewhat dissipated or improved by studied scientific crossing with top sires and matrons of other lines, thus securing better heads, more level backs, better tail carriage, stronger legs, and better conformation throughout. Few kennels, if any, have maintained any pure strain of Meron, Perrito, Si Si, Miniatura, Don Rubio, Don Apache or any other of the best known lines of yesterday. All have crossed these strains in attempting to produce better Chihuahuas. Yet, in most all of the outstanding kennels there are studs that carry through for four to six generations any one of the established bloodlines, thus perpetuating at least in part, the best characteristics of the best known strains.

It is unreasonable to expect or assume that any champion stud or outstanding stud of any strain should always and only sire get of his own quality. No sire throws all top puppies! However, when a certain cross results in a litter, the majority of which are show type puppies, it is well to repeat the breeding. Experiments are tedious and costly, yet new and better strains may be developed through years of careful selective breeding, eliminating all culls or undesirables in color and type. Few established strains breed true to color, except Meron, Don Rubio, and Miniatura where fawns and reds predominate.

It should be said here that registered kennel names do not guarantee strains of the same name; that is, La Oro Kennels do not offer a La Oro strain, but in this well-known kennel, the Si Si strain predominates; in the La Reina Kennels, the dominant strains are Don Rubio and Perralto; in the La Rex Doll, the old Perrito line is paramount; in the Audubon Park Kennels of Mrs. Chas. Dobbs, the Meron strain is exclusive; the Kinsman Kennels breed long coats entirely of the Don Sergio strain, etc.

THE SI SI STRAIN

From the foundation champion stud of this well-known strain have come more champions than any other Chihuahua sire—four champion males and seven champion bitches. Mrs. Vinyard, who owned Ch. Si Si Oro Principe, comments: "While his sons were not of such high quality as his daughters, his grandsons are much better in type, and his great-grandsons and daughters are showing creditably."

The greatest show winner of 1949 in Chihuahua males is a great-grandson of Ch. Si Si on the maternal side through Ch. La Oro Tortilla, and this male, Ch. La Oro Alino de Tortilla de Oro, carries on the Si Si tradition with notable success through his outstanding get.

The Si Si strain continues to produce typey little dogs with plenty of Terrier fire and showmanship, good heads, and particularly sound bodies with good legs. Perhaps this strain which originally combined the Perrito and Meron bloodlines, has done more for the aggressive movement of the Chihuahua than any other strain.

THE MERON STRAIN

This strain, long admired and sought after by Chihuahua breeders everywhere, has been preserved in its purity by Mrs. Charles Dobbs through her selective breeding. Her outstanding Meron studs, Ch. Little Meron III, IV, and X, and

An excellent study of type, following through from sire to son.
Left: INT. CH. LA ORO ALINO DE TORTILLA DE ORO (Sire)
Bred and Owned by Mrs. Anna B. Vinyard, Cincinnati, Ohio
Right: CHAMPION NANOBBY'S ALINO (Son)
Breeder-Owner: Mrs. Douglas Williams,
Belton, Texas

their progeny in numerous kennels, have perpetuated the fine Meron type, particularly in excellent domed heads and soft, expressive eyes which distinguish the breed from all other dogs.

It has been proven many times that double Meron breeding produces some of the best type Chihuahuas today, and a most notable cross still used extensively is that of sons and daughters of Ch. Little Meron IV with bitches and dogs of the pure Perrito strain, especially direct descendants of the famed Ch. Perrito II.

THE PERRITO STRAIN

Ch. Perrito II was without doubt the outstanding sire of that fine strain, and ten of his sons were registered in his name. Some of the smallest and most typey Chihuahuas ever known in this country have come from the early imports from Mexico, Carranza and Sonora, ancestors of this strain, the Meron, and others. The line has been crossed with nearly every strain known, and although few absolutely pure Perritos are now in existence unless they are to be found in the older breeding stock of La Rex Doll Kennels, the blood still flows in most of our outstanding stock today. There are few Chihuahuas that do not boast in a previous generation a close relationship with the early Perritos, especially the well-known son of Ch. Perrito X, El Feljo.

THE DON APACHE STRAIN

This well-known strain developed by Olive C. Grudier furnished the basic blood for her successful breeding. Don Apache was not a small dog (he weighed six pounds) but many of his progeny reflect his finer qualities plus refinements obtained through careful crossing, bringing to the show ring some of the best that have ever been shown. Don Apache was a grandson of the famous Si Si. A half sister of Apache's, Diana, was bred to Ch. Little Meron IV, producing Ch. Meronette and Ch. Meronella Grudier. The offspring of these bitches, bred to Apache, have produced the best in Chihuahuas and now carry on the Don Apache strain.

Ch. My True Love Grudier no doubt threw more puppies

of the true Don Apache type than any of the Apache sires existent today. Ch. Meronette Grudier produced but one puppy, Son of Meronette, to carry on the famed career of his mother, who was one of the most beautiful and typey Chihuahuas ever to be shown, and who perhaps possessed the most enviable record of show wins.

THE DON RUBIO STRAIN

The two divisions of the Don Rubio strain are generally recognized, namely the Chicago branch of the strain brought from the West Coast by Sylvia DeFrankie years ago and now continued through the offspring of Tiny Gretta in the Threlkeld Kennels; and the Brush's Don Rubio branch, largely perpetuated through Ch. Don Rubio Grudier, foundation stud of La Reina Kennels, and his outstanding son, Ch. La Reina's Half Penny. Some of the original stock of this better known branch of the strain is to be found in the kennels of S. S. Thorpe on the West Coast, where two sons of the famous Ch. Brush's Don Rubio were used as studs.

This strain is known for its smooth red coats, fairly good heads (better when crossed with Meron or Perrito) and sound bodies. In movement and showmanship they leave little to be desired. Deer type characterizes most of the Don Rubio puppies though cobby Rubios are not unknown. The cobby type is more common in the Chicago branch, as demonstrated in the get of the little Ch. Mark's Don Rubio.

Although Chihuahuas are seldom successfully bred for color, the varying shades of red are perhaps more often found in this strain than in any other.

THE MINIATURA STRAIN

Many of this well developed strain are found today in Southern Kennels, and some outstanding studs are kenneled in such quarters as Tressa Thurmer's. Mrs. Thurmer believes that the Miniatura strain should be crossed today with every other strain in order to obtain the best results in breeding. Her Ch. Thurmer's Little Toni Jo is one of the top studs in Miniatura blood. Old Sol Tinto, a foundation stud in Gro-

CHAMPION HERSHEY MUIR
Sired by Champion Lenardo Muir
Breeder-Owner: Elsie Muir Kennels,
Albuquerque, New Mexico

CH. ALFORDS BONITA RUBIA
Sire: Ch. Hound Shello.
Dam: Alfords San Antonio Rose
Breeder-Owner: Mrs. C. M. Alford,
Catoosa, Olkahoma

CH. DON MARCIANO COLA
Sire: Maria's Tobishi II
Dam: Pelina Marie Cola

TAR BABY'S UNO POCO
Sire: Alford's Tar Baby
Dam: Wee Pansy of Bertmount

ALFORD'S HERSHEY MUIR
Sire: Ch. Hershey Muir
Dam: Alford's San Antonio Rose
All owned by Mrs. Clara M. Alford, Catoosa, Oklahoma

sart's Kennels was also a "grand old man" of this strain, and many Miniatura get are from him.

Browns, reds, deep gold, and other dark solid colors predominate in Miniaturas. One of the best known studs of this strain was El Capitan Villa of El Gusto Kennels. He consistently sired small puppies of fine type. He himself was a tiny, red-brown male with all the typical Miniatura points. Though not so well known as the Meron or Perrito, this strain is a good combination of the two, and by careful breeding of the best that is left of it today, the Miniatura could be developed into something very fine.

THE LA REX DOLL STRAIN

Although "La Rex Doll" is a registered kennel name associated with Bertha Peaster for many years, the La Rex Doll strain of Chihuahuas is also a well established strain, almost all of the great sires of which are direct descendants of Sonora and Chiquelo. Ch. La Rex Doll Pee Wee, and Ch. La Rex Doll Chiquelo are two of the best known sires of recent years. Mrs. Peaster declares that this strain "comes true to type in every generation and litter. It is an accomplishment which has taken years of faithful breeding to line, unremitting thought, care and expense, and is an achievement English breeders are reputed to believe impossible—that is, to establish an individual and permanent strain in any one breed."

La Rex Doll Chihuahuas are known for their excellent heads, sound bodies, large eyes and ears—ears standing well out, and not straight as in the black and tan. Although the modern tendency seems to be slanting definitely toward the solid colors in Chihuahuas, La Rex Doll strain has in it many fine black and white marked and spotted dogs, and their popularity is not diminished. Probably every kennel in the United States has much La Rex Doll stock or blood in it, and from this strain have come many of the top Chihuahuas.

THE DON SERGIO STRAIN

This is the only established strain of long coats in America. The long coated Chihuahua has gradually but surely come into its own, and judges are now willing to place a really good long coat at the top if better than the best smooth in the show. Because at certain times of the year they are out of coat; because they are sometimes larger dogs, and preference (according to The A.K.C. Standard) is given to the smaller type; and because heavily fringed ears sometimes do not stand perfectly—the long coated Chihuahua has been at a disadvantage in the show ring. Now, however, more and more are being shown at all large bench shows, and they are meeting with popular favor. A number of exclusive long coat kennels now exist.

Many beautiful long coats have graced the ring in recent years, but too often they are of smooth coated parentage, and therefore throwbacks. It is believed that the Meron strain has produced more longs than any other strain with the exception of the Don Sergio. This is believable as the import Caranza, according to the best authority, was a true long coat with bushy tail. In breeding long coats of finer quality today, it is essential that puppies are the product of long coat matings, and better still, from parents and grandparents of long coat blood.

The purest strain of genuine long coats in America is that developed and maintained by Alpha Kinsman, the Don Sergio. Don Sergio's own puppies are few, but among them are five long coated champions. All of the Don Sergio's have ruby eyes, and long silken coats of chocolate and white. Although The American Kennel Club has long accepted the long coat as a definite division of the breed, a few older breeders still exist whose prejudices forbid the acceptance of the long coat as purebred. But the Don Sergio strain proves the purity of the long, for careful inbreeding and studied line breeding have maintained the very best in Chihuahua type in this strain—retaining all outstanding Chihuahua characteristics in disposition and temperament.

CH. RAYAL'S ROBINITO PEPINO, C.D., Long Coat Chihuahua, owned by Mrs. Arthur Booth of Gardena, California.

CH. WEEVILLE'S 'TIS SO TOO has proved his prowess as a stud, throwing his own typiness to his get. He is owned and handled by M. Patrick Slade.

CH. THEIN'S MIAMI KID (Thein's Connie Bay, Jr. ex Thein's Nani). He is owned by his breeder, Louise Thein.

NEED FOR BETTER QUALITY MALES

Perhaps it is an unaccountable situation, but it is true that male Chihuahuas of the past few years are not of the same high quality as many bitches that have been shown to the title. This is not to say that there are no high quality males available for stud service, but they are few in comparison with the many excellent bitches, and this fact is substantiated by the expressed opinions of some of our best toy judges. At the Chihuahua Specialty in Chicago, Mr. Alfred LePine, complimented with an entry of 109 Chihuahuas, commented after the judging: "I found the bitches furnished a little keener competition than the dogs. The quality was particularly high in most bitch classes."

Why, with so many male puppies born, are top males at such a premium? We are of the opinion that there ARE good males available, of all strains and combinations of bloodlines, but the exhibitor has been led to believe that the Chihuahua male shown and advertised at stud, must be of the very tiny type, and some of the best males, some of the finest studs, are never shown.

The smallest stud does not always throw the smallest puppies. To judge fairly as to the quality of a stud of any strain, one must examine the sire, grandsire, and even great-grand-sire if possible. If a large stud is from a small background, smaller and more typey puppies will no doubt be realized than from a tiny stud from a large background. For instance, though Don Apache weighed six pounds, many of his get were tiny and of the best type.

We do not advocate breeding large pet type, Chihuahuas that resemble Fox Terriers, but when a large dog has all the points of the accepted Standard in his favor, and comes from a small background of one of the better known strains, there is no reason why he should be eliminated from show and stud competition with the best. Though diminutive size is generally demanded in Chihuahuas and preference in the show ring is given to the tiny of the breed, soundness and

65

movement are of paramount importance in the advancement of the breed. ALL strains produce large and small Chihuahuas, but The A.K.C. Standard discriminates against the larger dog ONLY when the tiny is equally as good in every other point.

CHAMPIONS AND OUTSTANDING STUDS OF VARIOUS BLOODLINES

Special attention might well be given in this chapter to a number of fine studs of various bloodlines, not mentioned in paragraphs preceding this. In the State of Texas there is a pure branch of the Meron strain called the "Texas Meron" which furnishes foundation stock of high quality for Hood and Strong Kennels. Two outstanding studs are Ch. Mi Panchetto and his lovely chocolate son Ch. Strong's Cho Cho Mino. These are of double Meron breeding, direct descendants of the famed Ch. Little Meron III. Hood's Little Man Forty Three is another of the same strain.

Jarro Antonio, of Fairyland Kennels, is one of the few pure Perritos left, a direct descendant of the famous Perritos III, VI, and X. In the fourth generation of Jarro's pedigree are such famous Chihuahuas as Ch. Little Pedro and Ch. Peaster's Little Sonora and Ch. La Rex Doll Chiquelo. Jarro Antonio is not a show type dog, but has sired such excellent champions as Ch. Mark's Ita Beno and Ch. Shreves' Meron the Great; the first combining Perrito and Chicago Don Rubio strains, and the latter, Perrito and Meron.

Ch. Alford's Pedro La Shello, a sound chocolate miniature, sired by the famous show winner, Ch. Hound Shello, is a combination of several of the best known strains including Meron, Perrito, Brush's Don Rubio, and others.

Ch. Moss' Billy Boy of Gordineer Kennels combines the Don Apache, Meron and Perrito strains. He is one of those very rare studs that usually throws his own fine cobby type in puppies sired by him, and is producing some of the best of the breed when crossed with pure Meron.

Ch. Don Marciano Cola, Don Maquito Cola, and others carry on the famous Perralto line today. Marciano finished for the title and in the Oklahoma Kennels of Clara Alford

66

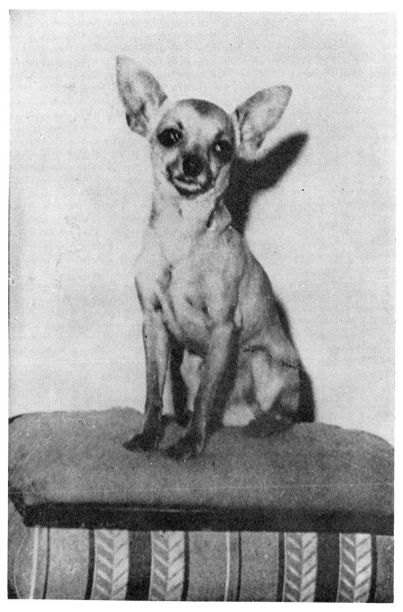
CHAMPION HOUND SHELLO
Selected by *Life* Magazine as one of the ten top dogs in the country. In 1947 he won more Best of Breeds than any other male Chihuahua, with 26 Best of Breeds, 18 Group placings and 2 Group wins.
Owned by Mrs. R. L. Melton, Houston, Texas

became a top stud. Maquito, of excellent championship quality, sired Ch. Vernadito Belle, Best of Winners at the 1949 Specialty Show in Chicago, and became one of the most aggressive studs in La Reina Kennels, which specialize in Perralto and Rubio lines.

An outstanding stud of a little known line of Chihuahuas, the Atom line from an old Indian in Pennsylvania a number of years ago, is Gordineer's Danny Boy, a black and tan 2¾ pounder in La Reina Kennels. Danny sired the two great Texas winners, Ch. David's Miguel, who was best of opposite sex in the Texas Chihuahua specialty show, and Ch. Pate's Tawanna, best of breed at the same show. A son of Danny, La Reina's Danny Chico, also became an outstanding stud.

Many others might be added to this meager list of fine Chihuahua studs but one can readily see that ALL strains and all combinations of strains produce occasional "flyers" and really top puppies. No kennel has ONLY the best, or ALL of the best, and all kennels have SOME of the best. Any reliable breeder can find some few among his breeding stock that he desires to eliminate as better dogs and matrons become available to him. Careful culling, breeding only the best that are available and eliminating as quickly as possible all that are not up to the Standard of the breed, will assure inevitable success and insure the production of better Chihuahuas in the years ahead.

CHAMPION DAVID'S MIGUEL
Sire: Gordineer's Danny Boy.
Dam: Poiciana Mia
Owner: Morris Lichtenstein
Corpus Christi, Texas

CHAMPION RATIONED SUGAR
Owned by Mrs. J. R. Dant, Coral Gables, Florida

Mrs. Anna B. Vinyard showing Ch. La Oro Damisela,
top Chihuahua for 1946

My Observations in Mexico

by Mrs. Anna B. Vinyard

Although I have bred Chihuahuas since 1930, it had never been my pleasure to visit Mexico, their country of origin until I was invited to judge all toys at the Spring Show of 1947. Not only did I accept the assignment with enthusiasm due to the honor bestowed on me but it was my expectation to learn a great deal about the breed and become acquainted with the fanciers of its native country. It was, therefore a great surprise that I was treated as an educator rather than as a student.

The people of Mexico, true to the tradition of all Latin American races, excel in politeness and treated me with the utmost courtesy. They seemed eager to learn about breeding principles of the United States and the Standard by which the Americans have developed their native breed. Just as the Chinese Chow was developed in England, the show type Chihuahua has been developed in the United States. This may seem strange to the novice but the principal dog-raising countries of the world, England, Germany and the United States have done more toward standardizing the points of the foreign breeds due to the fact that scientific breeding is in its infancy in many countries from which these breeds originate.

In Mexico, the advanced fanciers realize that the popularization of the Chihuahua has come about through the standardizing of the breed in the United States. Although this breed dates back to the days of Montezuma, little attention was paid to type. Size was the only consideration.

While I wish to be as charitable as possible toward Mexican dogs and their owners, on the whole they are not nearly as good type as in the United States and, coupled with bad show ring manners, made this shortcoming more obvious.

I was besieged with a barrage of questions as to the way in which we Americans have perfected the breed and the Mexican fanciers were eager to learn in order to perfect their own breeding programs. I have learned, or think I have learned, through past years of experience, and it was a pleasure for me to advise to the best of my ability, not only regarding breeding principles but as to the type which we consider ideal and thus help the little Chihuahua to come into its own in its native country.

It is true that my observations were confined to the dogs entered for exhibit and there are many in private homes, treasured as pets that will never be seen in the show ring and these specimens may or may not be superior to those which I had the pleasure of judging. However I believe that while the size and color may be desirable, their actual show points as we judge them, have been sadly neglected. To the orthodox Mexican, the Chihuahua is the only dog and he guards and prizes him most highly.

With the Mexican Kennel Association striving to adopt the methods of our American Kennel Club, we may look for a greater improvement in their native breed and that the Chihuahua will come into its own and I fear that American breeders within a few years will have to look to their laurels. I found in the officers and members of the Mexican Kennel Association, a general feeling of cooperative spirit to go along with our methods and principles, to obtain a strain embodying better type and more excellence in the canine population of the country south of the border.

CHAMPION LA ORO FARO
Sire: Ch. Oro De Ley
Dam: La Oro Pluma do Oro Romaro
Breeder and Owner:
Mrs. Anna B. Vinyard

I had occasion to visit the National Museum and view specimens of the early dogs of Mexico. They did resemble the Chihuahua as we know it today but were weak-legged and hump-backed. The size however, was very small. There seem to be two schools of thought in Mexico regarding the origin of the Chihuahua: one given to the popular belief of its origin as Mr. Denlinger has outlined, with reservations, in this book; the other headed by Professor Francisco Beltran, J., University of Puebla, Puebla, Mexico, a man who has spent much time in research and who, quoting from authorities as given in old books written by monks and Spanish explorers, gives as his opinion that the Chihuahua did not exist in the time of the Spanish conquerors but is the result of selective breeding from mongrel dogs brought over by the Spaniards.

Who is correct, the writer is not qualified to say but Professor Beltran's theory would surely rob the little Chihuahua of much of its romance.

73

CH. HURD'S HONEY BEE, a leading lady of the '70s, winning Best in Show at the Metro Mile Hi KC show in May 1969 under judge Clara Alford. Handler, Peggy A. Hogg. Co-owned by Max E. Hurd and Teddye Dearborn.

Into the 1970s

TO every Chihuahua fancier the outstanding show events of each year are the great Westminster Kennel Club show in New York held in February and the Chihuahua Club of America's Specialty usually held in the Midwest late in the year.

Entries at both events are likely to represent many of the breed's finest specimens existing at the time and competition is keen. In the compilations which follow it is encouraging to note that no one exhibitor has cornered the awards year after year. This speaks well for the universal quality of the breed, for when one kennel dominates the scene for any extended period of time, others tend to become discouraged and the breed regresses accordingly.

In the listings below are given the Best of Variety (BV) and Best of Opposite Sex (BOS) for the long coat and smooth coat varieties. For the benefit of those unfamilar with the divisions and awards determined under the rules of the American Kennel Club, the following explanation may be helpful. In breeds like the Chihuahua in which two types of coats are recognized the American Kennel Club divides the show classes into two varieties, one for each coat. The best specimen in its coat variety is named "Best of Variety." The best specimen in the other sex to the Best of Variety is named "Best of Opposite Sex."

75

At all-breed shows such as Westminster, both the smooth and the long coat Best of Variety winners compete in the Toy Group for further honors.

At separately held Specialty shows such as the Chihuahua Club of America Specialty, the four top winners—the smooth Best of Variety and Best of Opposite Sex, and the long coat Best of Variety and Best of Opposite Sex—come together in competition and a Best of Breed (or Best in Show) and a Best of Opposite Sex to the Best of Breed, are chosen. In the listing of the Specialty winners here, we have first listed the separate Variety winners, and have then separately listed the Best in Show (BIS) and Best Opposite to the BIS (BOS).

CH. FRAN-FIN TOM THUMB OF MOWERSON
Best of Variety, Madison Square Garden, 1956
Owner: K. Mowerson, Allendale, N. J.

Winners at the Westminster Kennel Club Shows
Smooth Coats

1959 BV - Ch. La May's Little Pistol, Mrs. M. Lazenby
     BOS - Thein's Dream Boy II, Dr. J. F. Landolfo and
           S. Weaver

1960 BV - Ch. El Juguete's Texanna, Mrs. D. Crouse
     BOS - Ch. Reedlynde El Caudillo, Mrs. J. Harris

1961 BV - Ch. Luce's Flash E. Gayla, Mrs. R. G. Luce
     BOS - Grosart's Tippee Tee, C. L. Turner

1962 BV - Ch. Davis's Merri Little Boy, H. T. Davis
     BOS - Ch. Thomas' Princess Tanya, I. E. Thomas

1963 BV - Bechtle's Chiquita, D. Bechtle
     BOS - Marsh's Koko Bean, Mrs. J. Marsh

1964 BV - Ch. Genes Champagne Girl, Dr. & Mrs. R. L. Miller
     BOS - Ch. Barnell's Rik O Shay of Misalou,
           D. J. Kutsugeras

1965 BV - Ch. Lockharts Liza Belle, Mrs. M. Lockhart
     BOS - Ch. Schaefer's Gheronimo, S. Nelles

1966 BV - Ch. Brecon's Individualist, S. Nelles
     BOS - Ch. Davis Sadie, R. R. Landau

1967 BV - Ch. Kappen's Sugar Creek Kid, M. Kappen
     BOS - Eden's Sumbeam, L. S. Potts

1968 BV - Ch. Kitty's Dixie Teardrop, A. L. Hughes
     BOS - Ch. Kitty's Little Joe Ruff, J. C. Meyers, Jr.
           and L. J. Richoux

1969 BV - Ch. Kitty's Miss Brag A Bout, Marquesa de Portago
     BOS - Ch. Kitty's Little Joe Ruff, J. C. Meyers, Jr.
           and L. J. Richoux

1970 BV - Ch. Varga's Tiajuana Brass, Mrs. E. Varga
     BOS - Ch. Cherrbob Chocolate Eclair, E. E. Majors

1971 BV - Ch. Jay's Speedy Gonzalles, Judy Kling
     BOS - Ch. Weeville's 'Tricia Too, M. P. Slade

Winners at the Westminster Kennel Club Shows
Long Coats

1959   BV   - Ch. Teeny Wees Kitten, K. E. Lacher
       BOS - Kaiser's Oliver, J. Kaiser

1960   BV   - Ch. Stephens' Sweet Maxie, E. M. Stephens
       BOS - Ch. Kaiser's Oliver, J. Kaiser

1961   BV   - Ch. Lane's Prince Rojalio, R. A. Lane
       BOS - Van Dussen's Black Beauty, Dr. R. Bittencourt

1962   BV   - Ch. Crouse's Fuzzy Wuzz, Mrs. D. Crouse
       BOS - Ch. Stephens' Top Hat, E. M. Stephens

1963   BV   - Lil Black Sambo of Nixon Acres, E. M. Atkinson
       BOS - Truedson's Candy, H. M. Truedson

1964   BV   - Ch. Gerharts Lady Luck, Mr. & Mrs. R. Sargeant
       BOS - Ch. True Dulls El Capitan, N. M. Truedson

1965   BV   - Ch. Forest View Wanda Pride, E. M. Atkinson
       BOS - Luces Red Pepper, Mrs. R. G. Luce

1966   BV   - Ch. Dartans Creme de Co Co Shroyer,
            D. L. and T. Y. Delaney
       BOS - Ch. Forest View Lucky Char, J. Rowe

1967   BV   - Ch. Dartans Creme de Co Co Shroyer,
            D. L. and T. Y. Delaney
       BOS - Ch. Forest View Lucky Char, J. Rowe

1968   BV   - Ch. Palmer's Little Phydeaux II, S. S. Palmer
       BOS - Ch. Palmer's Buff of Phydeaux, S. S. Palmer

1969   BV   - Virginia's Red Streak, Belcrest Kennels
       BOS - Luces Bettina, J. Turner

1970   BV   - Ch. Lucky's Mr. Terri Bubble of Oz,
            Mrs. P. H. Pittore and R. G. Racheter
       BOS - Ch. Terrymont Peach Parfait, H. & E. R. Terry

1971   BV   - Ch. Lucky's Junior Woodsman of Oz,
            H. Wm. Ohman and R. G. Racheter.
       BOS - Ch. Lucky's Miss Glinda of Oz,
            Kalibank Kennels and H. Wm. Ohman

CH. KOTTKE'S LITTLE SWEETY PIE, the top winning Chihuahua of the early 1960s. An all-breed Best in Show winner, she was bred and owned by Mr. and Mrs. George Kottke of Roseburg, Oregon.

CH. DAVIS' MERRI LITTLE BOY (Davis' Little Louigi ex Davis' Merri Lynn). He was Best of Variety at Westminster in 1962 and is owned by Helen T. Davis.

Top Winners at the 1970 Chihuahua Club of America Specialty

Above, CH. JAY'S SPEEDY GONZALLES, Best in Show. Bred by S. J. Clark, and owned and handled by Judy Kling of Chantilly, Virginia. Speedy finished to his championship from the puppy class with 3 Bests of Variety over Specials and a Group placement. He followed his BIS at the Chihuahua Specialty with win of ·Best Smooth at the 1971 Westminster.

Top on facing page, DARTAN'S MARTHA, golden fawn Long Coat, up from Bred by Exhibitor class to Best of Winners (5 points), Best of Variety and on to Best of Opposite Sex to the Best of Breed. Martha was also BOW for 5-points at the Chihuahua Club of Michigan 1970 Specialty. Bred and shown by Darwin L. and Tanya Y. Delaney, Essexville, Michigan.

Below on facing page, CH. DARTAN'S GOLDEN TANINA, Best of Opposite Sex to the Best Smooth at the 1970 CCoA Specialty. Tanina scored a 4-point major in her first show at the Chihuahua Club of Greater Milwaukee 1969 Specialty, and came back in 1970 to score another 4-pointer as BOS to the BIS. Bred by Darwin L. and Tanya Y. Delaney, she is owned by Ed and Kaye Dragan of Detroit.

81

Winners of Best in Show
and Best of Opposite Sex to the Best in Show
at Chihuahua Club of America Specialty Shows

1958 BIS - Ch. Lanewood's Mister Bill, Smooth Coat
        BOS - Ch. Mona Lisa of Quarter Moon, Long Coat

1959 BIS - Ch. Teeny Wee's Kitten, Long Coat
        BOS - Ch. Shroyer's Rickee Robin, Long Coat

1960 BIS - Bill's Cotton Candy, Smooth Coat
        BOS - Ch. Edens' Lucky Money, Smooth Coat

1961 BIS - Ch. Belden's Tammy La Grando, Smooth Coat
        BOS - Ch. Poole's Pride Pop Eye, Smooth Coat

1962 BIS - Ch. Edens' Timmy Lou, Smooth Coat
        BOS - Ch. Crouse's Texanna's Kid, M. Hollasay

1963 BIS - Ch. Pardue's Master Don, Smooth Coat
        BOS - Lillicos Jo Dee, Long Coat

1964 BIS - Ch. Langlais Goodie Goodie, Smooth Coat
        BOS - Ch. Rik O Shay of Misalou, Smooth Coat

1965 BIS - Averill's BoBo, Smooth Coat
        BOS - Ch. Luce's Channa, Long Coat

1966 BIS - Ch. Misalou's Little Rickey, Smooth Coat
        BOS - Ch. Dartan's Creme de Co Co, Long Coat

1967 BIS - Albet's Sam's Son, Smooth Coat
        BOS - Dartan's Pandora, Long Coat

1968 BIS - Beachy's Herfanita, Smooth Coat
        BOS - Ch. El-Mari Don Miguel, Long Coat

1969 BIS - Ch. Shroyers Rock Robin, Long Coat
        BOS - Ch. Hurd's Honey Bee, Smooth Coat

1970 BIS - Ch. Jay's Speedy Gonzalles, Smooth Coat
        BOS - Dartan's Martha, Long Coat

Winners at the Specialty Shows
of the Chihuahua Club of America
Smooth Coats

1958 BV - Ch. Lanewood's Mister Bill, Mrs. W. H. Skinner
     BOS - Ch. Tilley's Chee Chee, Miss G. Kottke

1959 BV - Duncan's Tamiama Blaze, T. C. Duncan
     BOS - Rowe's Wee Tesoro De Oro, B. & L. Rowe

1960 BV - Bill's Cotton Candy, T. W. Jenkins
     BOS - Ch. Edens' Lucky Money, Mrs. F. M. Bethea

1961 BV - Ch. Belden's Tammy La Grando, Barnell Kennels
     BOS - Ch. Poole's Pride Pop Eye, H. S. Ronkin and
           Mrs. J. Stuller

1962 BV - Ch. Edens' Timmy Lou, Mrs. H. M. Edens
     BOS - Ch. Crouse's Texanna's Kid, M. Hollasay

1963 BV - Ch. Pardue's Master Don, M. E. Baily
     BOS - Ch. Henderson's Lady Love Bug, C. C. Henderson

1964 BV - Ch. Langlais Goodie Goodie, B. Langlais
     BOS - Ch. Rik O Shay of Misalou, D. J. Kutsugeras

1965 BV - Averill's BoBo, T. E. Thurmer
     BOS - Ch. Tris Tans Fashination, O. C. Grudier

1966 BV - Ch. Misalou's Little Rickey, D. J. Kutsugeras
     BOS - Chookie's Lady Tinker Belle, B. & H. Gingerich

1967 BV - Albet's Sam's Son, Mr. & Mrs. R. W. Rullman
     BOS - Ch. Tris Tans Fashination, O. C. Grudier

1968 BV - Beachy's Herfanita, M. Beachy
     BOS - Ch. Hurd's Rickee Rue, M. E. Hurd

1969 BV - Ch. Hurd's Honey Bee, M. E. Hurd
     BOS - Ch. Varga's Tiajuana Brass, E. Varga

1970 BV - Ch. Jay's Speedy Gonzalles, Judy Fling
     BOS - Ch. Dartan's Golden Tanina, Edw. Dragan

CHAMPION DARTAN'S CHOCOLATE CHIPS, a deep chocolate Long Coat. Chips finished to his championship with four major-point wins. Best in Show at the 1970 Milwaukee and Metropolitan New York Specialties. Bred and shown by Darwin L. and Tanya Y. Delaney, Essexville, Michigan.

Winners at the Specialty Shows
of the Chihuahua Club of America
Long Coats

1958 BV   - Ch. Mona Lisa of Quarter Moon, G. J. Bart
      BOS - Ch. Michels' Elvis P., M. M. Michels

1959 BV   - Ch. Teeny Wee's Kitten, K. E. Lacher
      BOS - Ch. Shroyer's Rickee Robin, G. L. Shroyer

1960 BV   - Ch. Lanewood's Lilbit, Mr. & Mrs. D. O. Lane
      BOS - Ch. Lane's Prince Rojalio, R. A. Lane

1961 BV   - Ch. Thurmer's Lizetta, R. Vaenoski
      BOS - Ch. Ve-La's Delgotto, H. D. and B. A. Viele

1962 BV   - Ch. La Oro Alcancia de Oro II, A. B. Vinyard
      BOS - Ch. Shroyer's Rickee Robin, G. L. Shroyer

1963 BV   - Ch. Luce's Tony Tango, Mrs. R. G. Luce and
             Toni Powell
      BOS - Lillicos Jo Dee, E. and D. Lilloco

1964 BV   - Stonebraker's Rajo Abrigo,
             Mrs. K. W. Stonebraker
      BOS - Lehman's Victoria Lynne, J. Lehman

1965 BV   - Ch. Klein's Wee Twirt, D. B. Reiss
      BOS - Ch. Luce's Channa, D. L. and T. Y. Delaney

1966 BV   - Ch. Dartan's Creme de Co Co, Shroyer
      BOS - Ch. Douglas Pretty Boy, R. W. Douglas

1967 BV   - Dartan's Pandora, D. L. and T. Y. Delaney
      BOS - Ch. Gehlsen's Richardo Mio, E. L. Gehlsen

1968 BV   - Ch. El-Mari Don Miguel, M. H. Schmidt
      BOS - Florins Tink E Toot, L. E. McGowan

1969 BV   - Ch. Shroyer's Rock Robin, G. L. Shroyer
      BOS - Ch. Gochenours QP Doll, N. L. Schmalhauser

1970 BV   - Dartan's Martha, D. L. and T. Y. Delaney
      BOS - Ch. Shroyer's Rock Robin, Stephanie Reed

EARS large; held erect when alert; flaring 45 degrees in repose

HEAD well-rounded; skull "apple-domed"

NECK slightly arched; gracefully sloping into shoulders

BACK level, slightly longer than height; shorter back for males

EYES full, balanced; set well apart, dark; not protruding; light eyes in blonds allowed

NOSE moderately short; slightly pointed; self-colored or black; pink allowed for blonds

JAWS lean; teeth level; cheeks lean

SHOULDERS lean, well up, sloping to back

CHEST reasonably deep, plenty of brisket

FORELEGS straight, set well under shoulders; fine pasterns

FEET small, dainty; neither hare nor catlike; toes well-split-up, but not spread; pads cushioned; nails moderately long

TAIL moderately long; carried either up or out, or in loop with tip touching back; Longcoats with full plume; bobtail or tailless permitted if so born

HINDQUARTERS muscular; hocks well apart; neither in nor out; well-let-down; firm, sturdy

COLOR any color; solid, marked, splashed

SIZE: Weight, 1 to 6 lbs; 2 to 4 preferred

DISQUALIFICATIONS: Cropped tail, broken down or cropped ears. Longhairs—too thin coat that resembles bareness

RIBS somewhat rounded

PASTERNS fine

COAT—Smooths, texture soft, close, glossy, ruff at neck, scanty coat on head and ears; Longcoats, either flat or slightly curly; ears fringed; texture soft, feathering on feet; legs, with pants; large ruff on neck

Visualization of the Smooth Chihuahua standard. Reprinted with permission from Popular Dogs Publishing Company.

Official Breed Standard of the Chihuahua

(Approved by the Board of Directors of The American Kennel Club, January 12, 1954.)

SMOOTH COAT

Head—A well-rounded apple dome skull, with or without molera. Cheeks and jaws lean. Nose moderately short, slightly pointed (self-colored, in blond types, or black). In moles, blues, and chocolate, they are self-colored. In blond types, pink nose permissible.

Ears—Large, held erect when alert, but flaring at the sides at about an angle of 45 degrees when in repose. This gives breadth between the ears.

Eyes—Full, but not protruding, balanced, set well apart —dark, ruby, or luminous. (Light eyes in blond types, permissible.)

Teeth—Level.

Neck and Shoulders—Slightly arched, gracefully sloping into lean shoulders, may be smooth in the very short types, or with ruff about neck preferred. Shoulders lean, sloping into a slightly broadening support above straight forelegs that are set well under, giving a free play at the elbows. Shoulders should be well up, giving balance and soundness, sloping into a level back. (Never down or low.) This gives a chestiness, and strength of forequarters, yet not of the "Bulldog" chest, plenty of brisket.

Back and Body—Level back, slightly longer than height. Shorter backs desired in males. Ribs rounded (but not too much "barrel-shaped").

Hindquarters—Muscular, with hocks well apart, neither out nor in, well let down, with firm sturdy action.

Tail—Moderately long, carried cycle either up or out, or in a loop over the back, with tip just touching the back. (Never tucked under.) Hair on tail in harmony with the coat of the body, preferred furry. A natural bobtail or tailless permissible, if so born, and not against a good dog.

Feet—Small, with toes well split up, but not spread, pads cushioned, with fine pasterns. (Neither the hare nor the cat-foot.) A dainty, small foot with nails moderately long.

Coat—In the smooth, the coat should be soft texture, close and glossy. (Heavier coats with undercoats permissible.) Coat placed well over body with ruff on neck, and more scanty on head and ears.

Color—Any color—solid, marked or splashed.

Weight—One to 6 pounds, with 2 to 4 pounds preferable, if 2 dogs are equally good in type, the more diminutive is preferred.

General Appearance—A graceful, alert, swift-moving little dog with saucy expression. Compact, and with Terrier-like qualities.

SCALE OF POINTS

Head, including ears	20
Body	20
Coat	10
Tail	5
Color	5
Legs	15
Weight	10
General appearance and action	15
Total	100

LONG COAT

The long-coated variety of the Chihuahua is judged by the same standard as the smooth-coated variety, except for the following:

Coat—In the Long Coats, the coat should be of a soft texture, either flat or slightly curly, with undercoat preferred. Ears fringed (heavily fringed ears may be tipped slightly, never down), feathering on feet and legs, and pants on hind legs. Large ruff on neck desired and preferred. Tail full and long (as a plume).

Disqualification—Too thin coat, that resembles bareness.

SCALE OF POINTS

Head, including ears	20
Body	20
Coat	20
Tail	5
Color	5
Legs	10
Weight	5
General appearance and action	15
Total	100

DISQUALIFICATIONS

Cropped tail, broken down or cropped ears, too thin coat that resembles bareness.

CH. DARTAN'S PANDORA, homebred black and tan Long Coat bitch, owned by Darwin and Tanya Delaney. Pandora came from the Open class at the Chihuahua Club of America 1967 Specialty to go Best of Variety over a large class of Specials. She finished with two 5-point majors.

CH. DARTAN'S CREME DE COCO SHROYER, a top winning Long Coat Chihuahua of the mid-1960s. Finished to her championship with three 5-point majors, she scored many Best in Specialty wins, Group placements, and was Best of Variety at Westminster in 1966 and 1967. She was retired following her win of the Specialty of the Chihuahua Club of Michigan in 1967. Owned by Darwin L. and Tanya Y. Delaney.

The Blueprint of the Chihuahua

THE Chihuahua is a small dog, to be sure. But he is much more than merely small. He is of a definite and distinct type. That type is becoming better known every year, and it is no longer possible for a dog to get by as a Chihuahua just on the strength of his being little. The correct type is purely arbitrary, a convention arrived at by a long consensus of compromise. The Chihuahua is not devoted to any specific employments or uses which determine its structure.

Of course the Chihuahua must be structurally consistent, must not have a head too big for its body or vice versa, must be dainty and elegant, and must be sound. It may be demanded why soundness should be insisted upon in a variety not called upon for work. There are at least three reasons. One is the aforesaid structural consistency. To be a good dog, a Chihuahua must look like a dog and move like a dog. A crippled Chihuahua is unpleasant to look at; even persons who make no pretense of knowledge of canine structure recognize an unsound dog to be wrong, possibly without being able to define wherein or why it is wrong. However small the activity of a dog, however much it is

91

CH. RAYAL'S BLANCO Y NEGRO, U.D. has excelled in Breed showing and holds a Utility degree. Breeder and owner is Alberta E. Booth.

carried instead of being forced to walk, the movement of a dog is handicapped and impeded by his unsoundness. Thirdly, unsoundnesses are heritable; unsound parents beget unsound progeny.

Unsoundnesses must be especially guarded against, since they long threatened to destroy the breed. There are yet judges so prejudiced against the breed by its former unsoundnesses that they refuse to concede that sound Chihuahuas do or can exist. These men have only to look about them, but they still refuse to be convinced. "They are all unsound," they say. The fact is that unsoundness has been largely weeded from the breed, which has now had many generations of sound ancestry. We do not want unsoundness to return, and must sacrifice some degree of type and even of smallness when necessary in order to keep the breed sound.

92

Size

The matter of unsoundness has a considerable connection with size. For many years, breeders bred from small stock, regardless of its soundness, and even of its type. It is notorious that in extremely small dogs, soundness is difficult to maintain. This does not mean that all minute specimens are unsound, but it is intended as a warning that many of them are and it is even more necessary to consider their soundness than that of larger dogs.

Not only has the breeding from abnormally small and unsound dogs tended to unsoundness in the breed, but the effort to control size by under-feeding has aggravated the condition. It is surprising that breeders won't learn that the size of a dog is controlled essentially by its germ plasm, and that starvation of puppies has little effect upon the size the dog is finally to attain. However, it has a tremendous effect upon the dog's soundness. It cannot be expected that a malnourished puppy will develop into a sound and vigorous dog. The main fault is in the owners who pass over unsoundness because they do not recognize unsoundness when they see it—especially if it is the unsoundness of their own dogs. It has become a habit to dismiss the other fellow's dog as unsound, but one is prone to seek to absolve one's own dog of that charge.

Size is a matter that can be determined by the scales. All other things being equal, the best Chihuahua is the smallest one. But all other things are never equal, and a four or five pound dog that is typical and sound is always to be preferred to a tiny mite of one or two pounds that doesn't look like a Chihuahua and cannot move like a dog at all. Six pounds is the maximum limit for a show Chihuahua (although brood bitches of greater size may produce small show dogs), and four pounds is better than six for a show dog. It is seldom that one finds everything—smallness, type and soundness. If we must sacrifice one of the

93

three, extreme smallness must give way to type and soundness. Chihuahuas are not to be judged by the scales alone.

Evaluation of Faults

The ordinary living room provides quite enough space in which to evaluate the merits of a Chihuahua. The demands are so simple that it is not necessary to be a judge of dogs to know what is wanted and what is to be rejected. We must not look for perfection, for we shall not find it. It is better to have a sound table, one that does not wobble, on which to place the dog. The employment of a table may frighten a dog at first, especially if the top is too small or so smooth in its surface that the dog is liable to skid on it and be unable to keep his footing. It is essential that the dog be confident and happy in order to assure his style and aplomb.

It is also desirable, if it is intended ever to exhibit the dog in a dog show, to equip the dog with a very light collar and lead that he may get used to being led and controlled on the lead. Some judges will permit one to dispense with the lead while he examines the dog on the table; others will not. At all events, the dog will be expected to move on the lead for the examination of his gait and soundness. This equipment should never be ornamental; the plainer the better. Jeweled collars are not regulation. And never, never, never take a dog into a show with a harness. It is better not to use a harness at any time, anywhere. Besides pulling and loosening the dog's shoulders, a harness makes a dog ridiculous, and ornamental accoutrement detracts from the beauty of the lines of the animal.

You wish to examine your dog to the end of ascertaining just how excellent or inferior he may be as a specimen of his breed. It is the purpose of this chapter to enable you

94

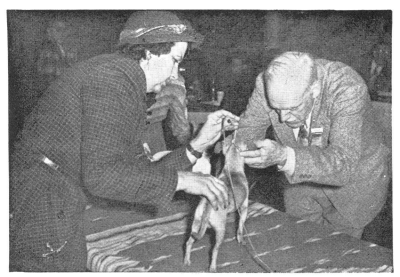

The late judge Alf LePine examining THURMER'S BAMBI at the 1949 Western Specialty on way to naming him Winners Dog. Owner, Tressa E. Thurmer.

to do this. However, we must make the reservation that the excellence of a dog is comparative. Under our examination, your dog is competing with the hypothetical absolute, with an ideal of perfection that can never be achieved.

The state of the Chihuahua fancy is such that you may win at some shows with a dog that you have concluded is inferior; on the other hand, you may lose with one that you have decided for yourself is very excellent indeed. It depends largely upon the competition that is met and even somewhat upon the ideals of the respective judges under whom the dog is exhibited.

With the foregoing considerations, or reservations in mind, let us place our dog on the table and look at him as objectively as possible to ascertain his degree of excellence, not in

CH. DARTAN'S BLAZON DRAGON, litter brother of Ch. Dartan's Golden Tanina. Bred by Darwin and Tanya Delaney, and owned by Edward and Kaye Dragan of Detroit.

CH. FARRISTON GOOD AND GAY, sire of ten champions. Bred and owned by Mrs. Homer V. Farris, New Hartford, Conn.

comparison with some other dog or dogs but with the absolute of perfection. It is to be remembered that a dog may be a very good Chihuahua indeed without conforming to the absolute ideal. There are few that even approximate it.

The Head

Let us first examine the head, not because it is the most important feature of the Chihuahua, but because it is the "index of the breed" and we cannot have a good Chihuahua without a good head. While we are unable to say that the head of the Chihuahua should be, in proportion to the remainder of the dog, as large as possible, yet it has a considerable width, and we do not remember ever having seen a Chihuahua with a head which we deemed to be too big for the body.

The first consideration of the head is its roundness of top skull. This roundness is of the skeletal structure and does not include the muscles of the cheeks, which should be flat or almost flat. The Chihuahua must never have an expression of a chipmunk with a nut in the corner of its mouth.

In the center of this top skull is to be found the "molera." This is perhaps the most distinguishing feature of the breed, and in plain English is "a hole in the head." It is due to the failure of the parieto-occipital suture to close, and in the human infant is known as the "fontanel" or "fontanelle," which usually in the human closes or disappears at an early age. In the Chihuahua, however, it persists usually throughout the life of the dog. In some specimens it gradually closes and cannot be found after a dog is three or four years old. If it is large enough in a young dog, it will probably be detectable throughout the life of the animal.

The failure of this fontanel to close is a sure test of the purity of the dog's blood, since the Chihuahua is the only breed of dogs that manifests the trait. The converse of this statement is not true, however. The absence of molera does not argue the impurity of the dog's blood, since the

97

sutures may close and the molera disappear when the dog is fully mature. Its presence is a characteristic feature—perhaps the most characteristic feature of the breed—and in competition its absence may be penalized despite the fact that the dog when younger may have had a molera and despite that it is purebred and known to be purebred.

This open suture, if found in any other breed of dogs would be considered a mark of unsoundness, since it leaves the dog that has it particularly vulnerable to blows on the head. The brain in the immediate area is but lightly protected and could be easily punctured by a light blow from a pointed instrument.

The molera serves no purpose except to differentiate the Chihuahua from any other kind of dog. It is a purely arbitrary demand upon the breed, and it would be just as logical to demand that the breed have two tails or six toes on each foot, or any other kind of abnormality. Happily, the Chihuahua is not exposed to rough treatment, and the molera, which if considered objectively would have to be classed as a defect, is not practically harmful, although it serves no purpose except to differentiate the breed from all others.

If your dog does not manifest this "hole in the head," especially if the dog is two or three years of age, do not conclude that the dog is not a Chihuahua at all. Its absence may count against him in the show ring, but it is not a cause for disqualification. If he has the "hole in the head," he is a purebred Chihuahua, however big he may be or however much he may fail in other particulars.

The muzzle is as small, short, and fine as possible. It is set low on the top skull, with a deep stop and considerable identation between the eyes. The top of the muzzle is parallel with the top of the skull, although the chief consideration is that it be short and fine. A long, strong, well filled up muzzle does not belong on such a skull and detracts from the symmetry of the head.

Teeth

The teeth in the ideal specimen are even; *i.e.,* the inner surface of the upper incisors overlap the outer surface of the lower incisors just sufficiently to play upon them. The teeth serve the Chihuahua merely to grasp its food daintily, and the exact formation of the teeth, assuming that they do not distort the expression of the face when the mouth is closed, is not of major importance. A clean, regular, and even set of teeth is of course desirable, but minute malformations of the mouth of the Chihuahua are not to be penalized so heavily as in the Terrier breeds, which employ their mouths in their struggles with their quarry, and in which strength and evenness of teeth are imperative.

The Chihuahua seems to inherit poor teeth, and in spite of a proper feeding program, including sufficient calcium, and an occasional removal of accumulated tartar, the teeth of the two or three year old Chihuahua often loosen and fall out and others rapidly decay. There seems to be an inherent weakness here, and the oldest and best known breeders have as yet discovered no remedy. So long as the teeth are even, not undershot or overshot, the absence of a tooth or two in a Chihuahua past two years of age should be overlooked by a judge and not penalize the dog.

A mouth much overshot, and especially an undershot one, can usually be detected without opening the mouth. The overshot mouth causes the expression to appear weak, and the undershot mouth gives the dog an appearance of truculence, which is quite foreign to the breed. This becomes a major fault and must be heavily penalized in the show ring, and it is very liable to reproduce itself in the progeny and grand-progeny of the dog that has it.

Commenting on the quality of Chihuahuas exhibited at the 1949 Specialty Show in Chicago, where he judged 109

CHAMPION PEARSON'S LITTLE STRUTTER
Sire: Pearson's Baby Chico. Dam: Pearson's Mabelita
Breeder-Owner: Mrs. E. L. Pearson, Summerland, Arizona

entries, A. Alfred LePine said, "I would say there has been a decided improvement in soundness and movement in the breed generally of late years. Heads are generally good with few bad ears present. But mouths could be better. I found some undershot, others overshot with a tendency to what is termed pig jaw. When this condition is present the under-jaw usually lacks substance and finish, with the receding underjaw giving a rather foreign look and not the true Chihuahua expression. We note this condition at times in other breeds where diminutiveness is desirable—underjaws some-times lack sufficient substance to permit teeth to come in without crowding, due to this lower jaw being too narrow. However, a little care in eliminating dogs with this tendency from breeding operations should correct this deficiency in the breed and aid the Chihuahua to secure its fair share of success in interbreed competition."

CHAMPION ALFORD'S BABY DUMPLING
Sire: Snootie (son of Ch. LaRey). Dam: Beaumanor Ardita.
Breeder-Owner: Mrs. Clara M. Alford, Catooska, Okla.

Eyes

The eyes of the Chihuahua are set wide apart, are large, but without protruding. They are soft and luminous, giving the dog an expression of gayety without aggression. They are set within the cheeks and rather high in the skull, on either side of the depression in the skull above the set-on of the muzzle.

The Standard says that the eyes should be dark, ruby, or luminous. Some breeders contend that the ruby eye and the molera are the two most distinctive features of the breed, but many Chihuahuas do NOT have the ruby eye. The ruby, or jeweled eye, glows like a ball of fire under certain light, and it was believed by the Aztecs that the ruby eye of the Chihuahua would serve as a light to guide the spirit of the Aztec to a place of safety in the Beyond. The ruby eye is

101

common to the chocolate Chihuahua, and many of the fawns and whites, while the dark eye matches the darker coats, and furnishes a striking contrast in the fawns and whites when it appears there. The amber eye is also acceptable in the fawn and red Chihuahua. Since color of coat is immaterial, we are forced to accept the eye color that goes with the respective coat colors. Dark, expressive eyes are always attractive, but light eyes are more tolerable with some coat colors than with others.

Ears

The ears of the Chihuahua should be large; we can almost say the larger the better, anyway noticeably and strikingly big. They are set on the corners of the skull and flare toward the sides, thus emphasizing the width of skull. They especially should not be vertical on the skull. They should be persistently stiff, giving the head the aspect of a moth about to take off in flight. Weak, tipped, or even drop ears are frequently found. They are not characteristic of the breed and should be heavily penalized, but they are not cause for disqualification. Earlier Standards were more lenient with drop ears, and even rose ears were included in the specification of one of the official Standards. With the improvement of the breed through persistent selective breeding, the qualifications have become more severe, and it is hard to get to first base with a lop-eared Chihuahua in any current major show. The Standard cites "broken down or cropped ears" as a warrant for disqualification.

This completes our description of the head, which is deceptively allotted but twenty points in the "Scale of Points" of the Standard. This twenty points is presumed to cover skull, muzzle, mouth, eyes, ears, and expression. While the scoring of dogs, the so-called score-card method of judging, is never conclusive, it is particularly undesirable in the Chihuahua, the head of which, including all its various features, is of much greater importance than to account for but one fifth of the whole dog. It is about the most important individual department of the dog and must, after soundness, be considered as paramount.

The Neck

The neck of the Chihuahua is in no way abnormal. It is somewhat longer than it appears, since the coat forms a kind of short ruff which stands off slightly, even in the smooth variety, and causes the neck to appear heavier and thicker than it is in fact.

The neck is exquisitely curved with a stallion-like crest, which is more especially marked on the dog than on the bitch. This is seldom apparent on a scrawny, half-starved little excuse for a dog whose sole merit is its diminutiveness. At all events the neck should not be concave and ewe-like. There should be no loose or surplus skin under the throat to impede the sweep of the eye over the clean lines of the animal.

The shoulder blades are long and well laid back, the neck fitting gracefully between them. They are at as nearly right angles as possible with the upper arms, which provides a considerable forechest. This is merely normal and good canine structure. The Chihuahua chest is of considerable width, with no stilty, narrow-fronted aspect.

Legs and Feet

The forelegs should drop straight from the elbows to the feet, with no curve or bow in the forearms. A suggestion of "give" or springiness at the pasterns is not to be penalized, but this does not mean that the dog may be "down on his pasterns." Loose elbows and the accompanying curved forearms were (and still are) so prevalent that some authorities,

103

including De Bylandt, long tended to accept them as correct. However, they are to be avoided in this breed as much as in other normal breeds of dogs. The bones of the forelegs should be as small and fine as possible compatible with the soundness of the dog.

The feet are usually rather more hare-like than cat-like; that is, they are slightly elongated rather than round. The exact shape is immaterial. What is important is that they shall be thick padded and not splayed. However, long toes, each toe distinctly developed, are characteristic of the breed. This is due to the nature of the nails, which should be noticeably large and strong, usually black, whatever the color of the dog. These claws are somewhat curved, and for exhibition purposes are left long and blunt, since they are one of the most marked features of the breed. These strong claws beat a veritable tattoo when the dog travels on a hardwood floor.

The claws may grow to such length as to hamper the dog's action, and may possibly curve back upon the foot. In such cases, the nails are to be shortened somewhat, but they should never be cut back more than is necessary to enable the dog to walk freely and without discomfort. The Standard fails to mention the strength and coarseness of these nails, stopping with the statement "with nails moderately long." It is not so much the length as the strength of the nails that marks the Chihuahua. Except for his small size and the molera, no single feature differentiates the breed from all others so much as do the strength and formation of the nails.

Of course they are a mere fancy point, as is so much else about the Chihuahua. They serve no useful purpose. They became a part of the breed convention from the probably erroneous assumption that the Chihuahua is (or is derived from) some wild, dog-like creature of the North part of Mexico which used its heavy claws as an aid in the climbing of trees and the burrowing of dens and caves in which it lived. Whatever the origin of the qualification, heavy claws are attributes of the Chihuahua as they are of no other breed of dogs.

104

CH. HURD'S BIT O'HONEY, Toy Group winner, bred and owned by Max E. Hurd and handled by Mrs. Hurd. Ch. Bit O'Honey was Best Brood Bitch in Show at the 1969 Chihuahua Club of America Specialty, where she was presented with her two top winning get, Ch. Hurd's Honey Bee and Ch. Hurd's Rickee Rue.

CH. HURD'S RICKEE RUE going Best of Opposite Sex at the Chihuahua Club of America 1968 Specialty under English judge, Mrs. Thelma Grey. Handled by breeder-owner, Max E. Hurd. Ch. Rickee was one of the Top Ten Chihuahuas in America for 1968 and 1969 (as compiled by Kennel Review).

Two pointed offspring of Ch. Char-Ell's El Dorado of Dartan, Best Stud Dog at the Chihuahua Club of America 1970 Specialty. Left, CHAR-ELL'S SUNDANCE KID, owned by Kitty Culbertson. Right, CHAR-ELL'S SANDPIPER, owned by Charles and Jewell Gonic.

Littermate offspring of Ch. Dartan's Blazon Dragon ex Dragan's Choo Choo scoring at Lima, Ohio 1970 show. Left, male, DRAGAN'S LITTLE BLAZE, BOS, owned by Dorothy Hodge, and right, DRAGAN'S MISS DEE DEE, BOB, owned by breeders Edward and Kaye Dragan and shown by James Lehman.

Chihuahuas often appear in the shows with light, dainty toenails, and we are unable to declare that they are not purebred. They are certainly not subjects for disqualification. However, other matters being equal, the specimen with coarse, heavy, somewhat curved nails is to be preferred.

The Body

Of the back and body, the Standard says: "Level back, slightly longer than height. Shorter backs desired in males. Ribs rounded (but not too much 'barrel-shaped')." The back is in fact that part of the spine between the withers and the pelvis, and should be short in both males and females.

The back is the part of the dog that transmits the power developed in the hindquarters to the forehand, which is not in itself a source of power at all. The economy of this power is not in the Chihuahua of any major importance, since the Chihuahua is seldom required to travel long distances under its own power or at top speed. It is important only as it conforms to good canine structure and satisfies the observer's eye.

The body, however, is not to be confused with the back. The body is comparatively long, measuring from the point of the shoulders at their junction with the upper arm to the extreme rear of the buttocks somewhat more than the height of the dog at the withers at the top of the shoulders. The Chihuahua must appear moderately low in comparison with its height. This length is derived from the forechest and the width of the quarters added to the length of back. However, the breed is not squat or low to the ground, like a Dachshund. It is just noticeably longer than it is high, but not excessively.

The ribs should be well sprung and capacious and the brisket should reach quite to the elbows or a little below. There should be but little tuck-up of the loin, just a tightening of the belly that prevents the appearance of obesity.

107

This substantial structure and capacity admittedly add something to the weight of the animal, though the Chihuahua is not to be judged by the scales alone. Vigor, symmetry, and soundness within small compass is our object, and if we have to sacrifice smallness by a few ounces in order to obtain a vital and complete dog, so be it.

The back line of the Chihuahua is level and horizontal from the withers to the pelvis, whence it slopes slightly to the set-on of the tail. Few are found with an absolutely level back. The tendencies are for the back to roach or for the dog to be higher at the pelvis than at the withers. This fault will be found to be not in the back itself but in the hindquarters and their absence of sufficient angulation.

The hindquarters should be muscularly substantial, although the skeletal structure remains fine. They are made up of long bones with considerable angulation at stifle and hock. The hock, in a natural stance should be vertical in, or just back of, a line dropped from the extreme point of the buttocks. The lower placed the hocks, the better.

Tail

The heavy tail is moderately long to long. It is carried in a sort of sickle, sometimes raised well above the horizontal. The Standard says of it "carried cycle," which means carried in a circle over the back. The tea-pot handle tail is rarely found and is not correct.

The Standard further says of the tail, "not tucked under," which can only have to do with temperament and timidity and not with structure. No confident dog of any breed tucks its tail. While the Chihuahua, at its best, is a gay, debonair, and fearless little fellow, we cannot reject a specimen just because of lack of confidence in a strange environment. Usually, a dog that tends to tuck its tail can, with a little encouragement, be made to pluck up its courage and carry its tail in a natural manner. The breed is not constitutionally shy or timid.

108

THURMER'S NEGRETA
Sire: Thurmer's Tito. Dam: Cookie
Owned by Tressa E. Thurmer,
Palatine, Illinois

THURMER'S MITZI   THURMER'S AZULADO BENITO
THURMER'S BLONDIE
Bred and Owned by Tressa E. Thurmer, Palatine, Illinois

Naturally short tailed or tailless dogs are sometimes, though rarely, found. The Standard makes provision for their acceptance, although a Chihuahua with a short tail (possibly because we are not used to seeing it) does not look quite right.

Among the disqualifications is listed "cropped tail," by which is probably meant a "docked tail." If a tail has been cleverly docked by a good surgeon it is almost impossible to tell from a naturally short tail. It is a question not likely to arise, since dogs with naturally short tails are so seldom encountered and those with artificially shortened tails even more seldom.

A Chihuahua characteristic is a slight flatness of the tail. This is the result of the coat rather than the structure of the tail itself. Indeed, the coat of the tail is a test of the correct coat of the dog as a whole. The coat does not part, but grows just a little longer on the sides than in the center, with the result that in running the tail between thumb and finger it appears to be slightly flattened.

Coat

Chihuahua coats are of two kinds—short haired and long haired. Short coated dogs are infinitely more numerous, and the long hairs are not often seen. They are, however, as eminently correct as the short haired variety. Beneath the coats, the two varieties are structurally just alike.

All kinds of short coats are found on Chihuahuas although there is one characteristic and correct kind of coat. This is a very dense, fur-like coat, very short and smooth over the head and ears, with a kind of short ruff over the neck and shoulders, shortening on the body again and longer on the tail. The dog should be free from naked or nearly naked areas, which are so often found on short haired toy dogs of other breeds. The Chihuahua coat is not close fitting, but rather tends slightly to stand away from the skin.

110

Who does she think she is, Miss America? CH. WETMORE'S GOLDEN GIRL, Smooth Coat and CH. FOREST VIEW SNOW WHITE FLUFF, Long Coat, owned by Mrs. Homer V. Farris.

Togetherness in a salad bowl. FARRISTON WEE MUFFIE with her daughter CH. FARRISTON FEATHERS, owned by Mrs. Homer V. Farris.

CH. CARR'S ROSEBUD, owned and shown by Jerry Rigden.

The hair colors are absolutely immaterial. Black, white, red, blue, gray, fawn, chocolate, liver, cream, and tan are equally acceptable. Nor does the distribution of the colors make any difference. There is no technical choice between solid colors and piebalds or parti-colors. Although there may be a personal choice among the colors, such personal equations are not presumed to affect the excellence of the dog. The color of the nose varies with the color of the coat, with which it is in keeping.

Movement

We have surveyed the dog rather completely, except for the final test of its action and ability to move correctly. If the construction of the dog is adequate it will hardly fail in its action. However, let us place the little fellow on the floor with light collar and lead and, with somebody to handle and guide it, have it led away from us and back toward us.

As the dog moves away, the hocks should be kept vertical, turning neither in nor out. The stride should be long and flexible, alert and sure. There should be no uncertainty or wobble from side to side, no sign of weakness.

As he returns toward the observer, the front legs should be parallel one to the other. He should not weave or paddle. A weaving action is indicative of loose shoulders. A paddling action, seldom found in this breed, indicates too strong an attachment of the shoulder blades.

It is idle to expect that sureness and vigor of action in a Chihuahua that is to be found in a good gaited Doberman Pinscher or even a Miniature Pinscher. However, weaknesses and any tendency to be crippled must set a dog back tremendously. A good Chihuahua requires to be sound in his action, and able to follow his owner on long walks.

Something must be said about style. While a dog may show himself high headed and alert on one day and cringe in terror on the following day, he can usually be made so

Two Grudier Puppies
Owned by Mrs. Olive C. Grudier,
Columbus, Ohio

confident that he is never afraid. No matter how excellent
a Chihuahua may be structurally, when he crawls on his

belly and shivers or refuses to permit himself to be examined on the table we cannot expect a judge to place him over a somewhat worse dog that is showing for all he is worth. In such a case the judge is not to be blamed. Rather the blame should fall on the dog, or better yet on the owner who has failed to train and condition his dog for the show ring.

THURMER'S RAMONA

THURMER'S DOLLY, THURMER'S BETTY and THURMER'S CINDY
Starting out on their show career
Bred and Owned by Mrs. Tressa E. Thurmer, Palatine, Ill.

Special Care of the Chihuahua

THE maintenance and management of the Chihuahua are little different from the careful husbandry of other kinds of small dogs, though varying somewhat from those of larger breeds.

First and foremost is the matter of size in its relation to food. The tendency to try to stunt the Chihuahua and to keep it small by withholding nutritious food from it is the greatest mistake a dog breeder can make. First, it fails of its purpose; and secondly, it weakens the dog, making it unhealthy and unsound. The size to which a dog is to grow is determined by its breeding and not to any great extent through its feeding. There is no known method by which a dog intended to grow to a certain size can be kept small.

Because the Chihuahua is small, there is a general tendency to consider it delicate and that its appetite requires to be pampered. This is a mistaken concept, since the Chihuahua is not more likely to be frail and delicate than any other breed of dogs—unless by wrong treatment he has been made delicate.

Like all dogs, the Chihuahua requires a highly nitrogenous diet. Meat with a considerable fat content is the best possible

117

CHAMPION BONNIE TA-DO-DUSTO
Champion Long-coated Variety
Owned by Samuel E. Harrison,
Greenville, S. C.

food. This should be ground or cut fine to enable the dog to swallow it. A plentiful supply of the various vitamins and minerals is also essential. Don't stint on these substances or neglect them, if it is desired to keep the Chihuahua vigorous.

The Chihuahua does not eat as much as a Saint Bernard, of course. But a small dog, pound for pound, will eat more than a large one. It is impossible to say exactly how much food to give a Chihuahua, since some dogs of a given size require more food than others; but a good rule is to give the dog all the food he will clean up readily. It is true that a few dogs will overeat, lay on fat, and become obese. This is to be avoided, and such dogs should have their rations limited. They should not be permitted to grow fat and sluggish. Such dogs are exceptions. The general rule is that the Chihuahua shall be given, within reason, all he wants to eat.

Above all, his food should be nutritious. Milk and shredded wheat makes a suitable breakfast; plenty of ground beef suffices for his dinner. Vegetables are not necessary, and, if fed at all, should be puréed for so small a dog. Their fiber content would be a burden to his intestinal tract.

Particular judgment must be used in the dosage of medicine for so small a dog. It is best to dispense with the use of medicines at all, unless it is absolutely necessary. Once a dog is free from worms, it is sheer negligence on the part of the owner that he shall gather a fresh crop of them. Never give a vermifuge unless you are sure that the dog has worms. Vermifuges are irritants to the intestines and probably harm more dogs than do the worms they are designed to expel. Keep the dog well and it will be unnecessary to resort to medication to cure him.

It is positively harmful to carry a Chihuahua around on a cushion and deprive him of the exercise he needs. An adequately nourished Chihuahua can follow under his own power well nigh anywhere his owner chooses to walk. Plenty of exercise in the open air is beneficial for him; he enjoys it; and he should be permitted to take it.

A dog that doesn't get enough to eat is of course loath

SHROYER'S MARTO II, SHROYER'S GAY GAL, LA NELLETA ARNOLD
Shroyer's Indian Lake Kennels, Lakeview, Ohio

HAMLEY'S LITTLE WONDER, MERRICK'S ANISE,
HAMLEY'S LUCKY LINDA, GENTLEMAN KO KO
Owner: Mrs. Mildred Le Gate, Watonga, Oklahoma

Chihuahuas
Bred and Owned by Tressa E. Thurmer, Palatine, Illinois

to exercise, but a Chihuahua well fed and in good health can travel at a steady pace all day. There is something wrong with any dog that fails to frisk and show activity.

There is nothing abnormal in the Chihuahua's need to be kept reasonably warm. He is a very small dog of smooth coat, not large enough to conserve body heat and seldom fed enough to develop such body heat. A well fed dog is not particularly sensitive to the cold, but gets cold quicker.

It is not the Chihuahua's Mexican origin but his small size that causes him to require some consideration for his temperature. His quarters should be maintained at a comfortable temperature between sixty and seventy-five degrees, and he should not be taken out of doors in extremely severe weather without a jacket or sweater. However, if he is well fed, no undue precautions are necessary. He is hardier than you believe.

Up to a dozen Chihuahuas can be kept together in a single room of the house without segregation. Only if the inmates of a kennel are very numerous is it necessary to establish separate quarters for Chihuahuas. The breed is not quarrelsome and a great many dogs can be quartered

121

THURMER'S ALOHA
Sire: Pates Toni Jo. Dam: McIntyres Chiquita
Puppies sired by Thurmers Malvado Tito
Owner: Mrs. Monzell Stoar, Chicago, Illinois

together. Even if they do get into a scrap, it is seldom that any of them is injured.

Of course it is necessary to separate bitches in heat from all male dogs except the one to which they are to be bred, else it is impossible to keep track of the pedigrees correctly. Bitches due to whelp, whelping, or with young puppies are best separated from the other inmates of the kennel, lest they be disturbed and their puppies injured. A commodious shipping crate, either made at home or purchased ready-made, provides an adequate temporary home for such bitches. No breed is easier to house.

With adequate clean quarters, exercise, and plenty of good sound food, this above all, a small or large number of Chihuahuas can thrive in little space.

Chihuahua puppies should be whelped in a temperature of 80 to 85 degrees, and special care must be given each puppy on its arrival to insure survival. Often the bitch will totally disregard her offspring, not even breaking the sack or biting the cord. The breeder must await the arrival of each puppy, cut the cord, rub the puppy and place it on an electric pad or hot water bottle, unless the mother will allow it to nurse when placed to her breast. The exceptionally tiny puppy may need special attention and hand feeding (half and half canned milk and warm water) for the first two or three days, to supplement the small amount of milk it may get from its mother, especially when the litter numbers four or five and other puppies are larger and stronger. Very few Chihuahua matrons care for their puppies at birth, and these few considerations are essential to the novice, if the tiny babies are to survive.

The standard food for nursing mothers and weaning puppies in all Chihuahua kennels is canned milk (diluted one-half with warm water) and Pablum, with a small amount of light Karo syrup added. The puppies will ordinarily begin to eat with the mother about the age of three or four weeks, and should be completely weaned at six or seven weeks of age. At that age they should be eating a small amount of lean ground beef (raw) along with the milk and Pablum mixture. An occasional graham cracker is a splendid addition to the feeding program which includes three meals a day until six months of age. Then two a day until a year old, when the adult schedule of one meal a day may satisfactorily be inaugurated.

In preparing the Chihuahua for the show ring, the usual procedure is employed: teeth are cleaned, nails are trimmed, whiskers are cut, and the dog is bathed and brushed. No coat dressing is necessary, as a well fed Chihuahua is always in good coat. The usual training to a lead and posing are essential and a dog of this breed must WALK, the same as any other dog, for action is important. A timid, cringing dog should NOT be shown!

Although the Chihuahua is particularly healthy and escapes many of the common diseases of canines, he IS subject to distemper when exposed and inoculation is suggested for the protection of the show dog, and in fact, all valuable pet and kennel stock. Your veterinarian will suggest the most satisfactory inoculation in your locality.

123

CANADIAN, AMERICAN, MEXI-CAN and BERMUDIAN CHAM-PION BRECON'S INDIVIDUALIST, Group and Best in Show winner and sire of many champions, pictured in his win of the Smooth Coat Variety at Westminster in 1966 under judge Haskell Schuffman, with Lorraine Heichel handling. Owned by Sandra Nelles, Brecon Kennels, Unionville, Ontario, Canada.

CH. BRECON'S BLACKADOT, a 1968 Toy Group winner at only 8-months-old. Owner, Sandra Nelles.

124

INT. CH. SEGGIEDEN JUPITER, show luminary of the late 1950s owned by Lady Margaret Drummond-Hay of Perth, Scotland. Jupiter, linebred from famous American champions Sweet Briar Don, Rhodes Tiny Tim and Rhodes Tiny Tim, Jr., was sire of champions in many countries, including Ch. Seggieden Tiny Mite, one of the all-time greats of the breed in England.

WINTERLEA LITTLEDENE TWIGGY, tiny Challenge Certificate winner, bred and owned by Mrs. Marjorie Money, England. Mrs. Money also breeds Chinese Crested Dogs.

THURMER'S LITTLE NEETA

Say it with Chihuahuas

Upon the occasion of Madam Adalina Patti's farewell appearance in Mexico, the then President of the Republic, Gen. Porferio Diaz, honored her with a reception and presented her with a magnificent bouquet of flowers. Hidden among the blossoms (as if one of them) the great diva found a tiny Chihuahua dog. Of course, in consideration of both the donor and the recipient, the specimen was a magnificent one and, despite its minute size, thoroughly sound. Mme. Patti adopted the animal at once, named it Bonito, and carried it with her wherever she went all over the world. Bonito lived for a long span of years, and after his death, Mme. Patti obtained other Chihuahuas. This was before the time that Chihuahuas were well known outside Mexico, and the dogs of the great singer were a sensation wherever she went.

The pretty gesture of enclosing a gift Chihuahua in a bunch of flowers is not an unusual custom in Mexico, where grace and sentiment, more than in other parts of the world, go hand in hand with practicality. It is one that could well be adopted in the United States.

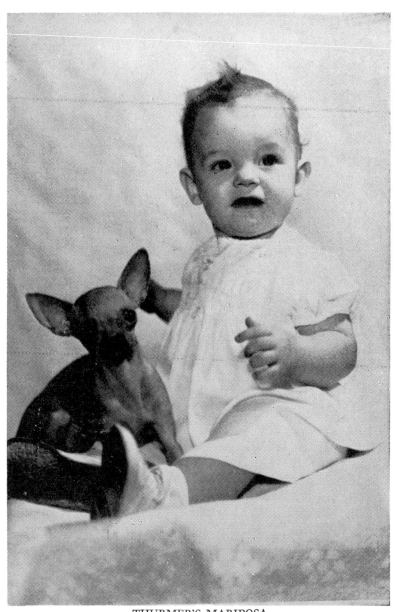

THURMER'S MARIPOSA

Part II

GENERAL CARE AND TRAINING OF YOUR DOG

by
Elsworth S. Howell
Milo G. Denlinger
A. C. Merrick, D.V.M.

Introduction

THE normal care and training of dogs involve no great mysteries. The application of common sense and good judgment is required, however. The pages that follow distill the combined experience and knowledge of three authorities who have devoted most of their lives to dogs.

Milo Denlinger wrote many books out of his rich and varied experience as a breeder, exhibitor and owner of a commercial kennel. Elsworth Howell has been a fancier since young boyhood and claims intimate knowledge of 25 different breeds; he is an American Kennel Club delegate and judge of the sporting breeds. Dr. A. C. Merrick is a leading veterinarian with a wide practice.

The chapter on "Training and Simple Obedience" covers the basic behavior and performance every dog should have to be accepted by your friends, relatives, neighbors and strangers. The good manners and exercises described will avoid costly bills for damage to the owner's or neighbor's property and will prevent heartbreaking accidents to the dog and to the people he meets. The instructions are given in simple, clear language so that a child may easily follow them.

"The Exhibition of Dogs" describes the kinds of dog shows, their classes and how an owner may enter his dog and show it. If one practices good sportsmanship, shows can be enjoyable.

The chapter on feeding offers sound advice on feeding puppies, adult dogs, the stud dog and the brood bitch. The values of proteins, carbohydrates, fats, minerals and vitamins in the dog's diet are thoroughly covered. Specific diets and quantities are not given because of the many variations among dogs, even of the same breed or size, in their individual needs, likes, dislikes, allergies, etc.

"The Breeding of Dogs" contains the fundamental precepts everyone who wishes to raise puppies should know. Suggestions for choosing a stud dog are given. The differences among outcrossing, inbreeding and line breeding are clearly explained. Care tips for the pregnant and whelping bitch will be found most helpful.

The material on "External Vermin and Parasites" gives specific treatments for removing and preventing fleas, lice, ticks and flies. With today's wonder insecticides and with proper management there is no excuse for a dog to be infested with any of these pests which often cause secondary problems.

"Intestinal Parasites and Their Control" supplies the knowledge dog owners must have of the kinds of worms that invade dogs and the symptoms they cause. While drugs used for the removal of these debilitating dog enemies are discussed, dosages are not given because it is the authors' and publisher's belief that such treatment is best left in the hands of the veterinarian. These drugs are powerful and dangerous in inexperienced hands.

The chapter on "Skin Troubles" supplies the information and treatments needed to recognize and cure these diseases. The hints appearing on coat care will do much to prevent skin problems.

One of the most valuable sections in this book is the "instant" advice on "FIRST AID" appearing on pages 95-98. The publisher strongly urges the reader to commit this section to memory. It may save a pet's life.

The information on diseases will help the dog owner to diagnose symptoms. Some dog owners rush their dogs to the veterinarian for the slightest, transitory upsets.

Finally, the chapters on "Housing for Dogs" and "Care of the Old Dog" round out this highly useful guide for all dog lovers.

Training and
Simple Obedience

E VERY DOG that is mentally and physically sound
can be taught good manners and simple obedience by any normal
man, woman, or child over eight years old.

Certain requirements must be met by the dog, trainer and the
environment if the training is to be enjoyable and effective. The
dog must be rested and calm. The trainer must be rested, calm,
gentle, firm, patient and persistent. The training site should be
dry, comfortable and, except for certain exercises, devoid of distrac-
tions.

Proper techniques can achieve quick and sure results. Always
use short, strong words for commands and always use the *same* word
or words for the same command. Speak with authority; never
scream or yell. Teach one command or exercise at a time and make
sure the dog understands it and performs it perfectly before you
proceed to the next step. Demand the dog's undivided attention;
if he wavers or wanders, speak his name or pat him smartly or
jerk his leash. Use pats and praise plentifully; avoid tidbit training
if at all possible because tidbits may not always be available in
an emergency and the dog will learn better without them. Keep
lessons short; when the dog begins to show boredom, stop and
do not resume in less than two hours. One or two ten-minute
lessons a day should be ample, especially for a young puppy. Dogs
have their good and bad days; if your well dog seems unduly lazy,

tired, bored or off-color, put off the lesson until tomorrow. Try to make lessons a joy, a happy time both for you and the dog, but do demand and get the desired action. Whenever correction or punishment is needed, use ways and devices that the dog does not connect with you; some of these means are given in the following instructions. Use painful punishment only as a last resort.

"NO!"

The most useful and easily understood command is "NO!" spoken in a sharp, disapproving tone and accompanied with a shaking finger. At first, speak the dog's name following with "NO!" until the meaning of the word—your displeasure—is clear.

"COME!"

Indoors or out, let the dog go ten or more feet away from you. Speak his name following at once with "COME!" Crouch, clap your hands, pick up a stick, throw a ball up and catch it, or create any other diversion which will lure the dog to you. When he comes, praise and pat effusively. As with all commands and exercises repeat the lesson, until the dog *always* comes to you.

THE FIRST NIGHTS

Puppies left alone will bark, moan and whine. If your dog is not to have the run of the house, put him in a room where he can do the least damage. Give him a Nylabone and a strip of beef hide (both available in supermarkets or pet shops and excellent as teething pacifiers). A very young puppy may appreciate a loud-ticking clock which, some dog trainers say, simulates the heart-beat of his former litter mates. Beyond providing these diversions, grit your teeth and steel your heart. If in pity you go to the howling puppy, he will howl every time you leave him. Suffer one night, two nights or possibly three, and you'll have it made.

The greatest boon to dog training and management is the wooden or wire crate. Any two-handed man can make a ⅜" plywood crate. It needs only four sides, a top, a bottom, a door on hinges and

6

with a strong hasp, and a fitting burlap bag stuffed with shredded newspaper, cedar shavings or 2" foam rubber. Feed dealers or seed stores should give you burlap bags; be sure to wash them thoroughly to remove any chemical or allergy-causing material. The crate should be as long, as high and three times as wide as the dog will be full grown. The crate will become as much a sanctuary to your dog as a cave was to his prehistoric ancestor; it will also help immeasurably in housebreaking.

HOUSEBREAKING

The secret to housebreaking a healthy normal dog is simple: take him out every hour if he is from two to six months old when you get him; or the first thing in the morning, immediately after every meal, and the last thing at night if he is over six months.

For very young puppies, the paper break is indicated. Lay eight or ten layers of newspapers in a room corner most remote from the puppy's bed. By four months of age or after two weeks in a new home if older, a healthy puppy should not need the paper *IF* it is exercised outdoors often and *IF* no liquid (including milk) is given after 5 P.M. and *IF* it is taken out not earlier than 10 P.M. at night and not later than 7 A.M. the next morning.

When the dog does what it should when and where it should, praise, praise and praise some more. Be patient outdoors: keep the dog out until action occurs. Take the dog to the same general area always; its own traces and those of other dogs thus drawn to the spot will help to inspire the desired action.

In extreme cases where frequent exercising outdoors fails, try to catch the dog in the act and throw a chain or a closed tin can with pebbles in it near the dog but not on him; say "NO!" loudly as the chain or can lands. In the most extreme case, a full 30-second spanking with a light strap may be indicated but be sure you catch the miscreant *in the act*. Dog memories are short.

Remember the crate discussed under "THE FIRST NIGHTS." If you give the dog a fair chance, he will NOT soil his crate.

Do not rub his nose in "it." Dogs have dignity and pride. It is permissible to lead him to his error as soon as he commits it and to remonstrate forcefully with "NO!"

7

COLLAR AND LEASH TRAINING

Put on a collar tight enough not to slip over the head. Leave it on for lengthening periods from a few minutes to a few hours over several days. A flat collar for shorthaired breeds; a round or rolled collar for longhairs. For collar breaking, do NOT use a choke collar; it may catch on a branch or other jutting object and strangle the dog.

After a few days' lessons with the collar, attach a heavy cord or rope to it without a loop or knot at the end (to avoid snagging or catching on a stump or other object). Allow the dog to run free with collar and cord attached a few moments at a time for several days. Do not allow dog to chew cord!

When the dog appears to be accustomed to the free-riding cord, pick up end of the cord, loop it around your hand and take your dog for a walk (not the other way around!). DON'T STOP WALKING if the dog pulls, balks or screams bloody murder. Keep going and make encouraging noises. If dog leaps ahead of you, turn sharply left or right whichever is *away* from dog's direction— AND KEEP MOVING! The biggest mistake in leash training is stopping when the dog stops, or going the way the dog goes when the dog goes wrong. You're the leader; make the dog aware of it. This is one lesson you should continue until the dog realizes who is boss. If the dog gets the upper leg now, you will find it difficult to resume your rightful position as master. Brutality, no; firmness, yes!

If the dog pulls ahead, jerk the cord—or by now, the leash— backward. Do not pull. Jerk or snap the leash only!

JUMPING ON PEOPLE

Nip this annoying habit at once by bumping the dog with your knee on his chest or stepping with authority on his rear feet. A sharp "NO!" at the same time helps. Don't permit this action when you're in your work clothes and ban it only when dressed in glad rags. The dog is not Beau Brummel, and it is cruel to expect him to distinguish between denim and silk.

8

THE "PROBLEM" DOG

The following corrections are indicated when softer methods fail. Remember that it's better to rehabilitate than to destroy.

Biting. For the puppy habit of mouthing or teething on the owner's hand, a sharp rap with a folded newspaper on the nose, or snapping the middle finger off the thumb against the dog's nose, will usually discourage nibbling tactics. For the biter that means it, truly drastic corrections may be preferable to destroying the dog. If your dog is approaching one year of age and is biting in earnest, take him to a professional dog trainer and don't quibble with his methods unless you would rather see the dog dead.

Chewing. For teething puppies, provide a Nylabone (trade mark) and beef hide strips (see "THE FIRST NIGHTS" above). Every time the puppy attacks a chair, a rug, your hand, or any other chewable object, snap your finger or rap a newspaper on his nose, or throw the chain or a covered pebble-laden tin can near him, say "NO!" and hand him the bone or beef hide. If he persists, put him in his crate with the bone and hide. For incorrigible chewers, check diet for deficiencies first. William Koehler, trainer of many movie dogs including *The Thin Man's* Asta, recommends in his book, *The Koehler Method of Dog Training,* that the chewed object or part of it be taped crosswise in the dog's mouth until he develops a hearty distaste for it.

Digging. While he is in the act, throw the chain or noisy tin can and call out "NO!" For the real delinquent Koehler recommends filling the dug hole with water, forcing the dog's nose into it until the dog thinks he's drowning—and he'll never dig again. Drastic perhaps, but better than the bullet from an angry neighbor's gun, or a surreptitious poisoning.

The Runaway. If your dog wanders while walking with you, throw the chain or tin can and call "COME!" to him. If he persists, have a friend or neighbor cooperate in chasing him home. A very long line, perhaps 25 feet or more, can be effective if you permit the dog to run its length and then snap it sharply to remind him not to get too far from you.

9

Car Chasing. Your dog will certainly live longer if you make him car-wise; in fact, deathly afraid of anything on wheels. Ask a friend or neighbor to drive you in *his* car. Lie below the windows and as your dog chases the car throw the chain or tin can while your neighbor or friend says "GO HOME!" sharply. Another method is to shoot a water pistol filled with highly diluted ammonia at the dog. If your dog runs after children on bicycles, the latter device is especially effective but may turn the dog against children.

The Possessive Dog. If a dog displays overly protective habits, berate him in no uncertain terms. The chain, the noisy can, the rolled newspaper, or light strap sharply applied, may convince him that, while he loves you, there's no percentage in overdoing it.

The Cat Chaser. Again, the chain, the can, the newspaper, the strap—or the cat's claws if all else fails, but only as the last resort.

The Defiant, or Revengeful, Wetter. Some dogs seem to resent being left alone. Some are jealous when their owners play with another dog or animal. Get a friend or neighbor in this case to heave the chain or noisy tin can when the dog relieves himself in sheer spite.

For other canine delinquencies, you will find *The Koehler Method of Dog Training* effective. William Koehler's techniques have been certified as extremely successful by directors of motion pictures featuring dogs and by officers of dog obedience clubs.

OBEDIENCE EXERCISES

A well-mannered dog saves its owner money, embarrassment and possible heartbreak. The destruction of property by canine delinquents, avoidable accidents to dogs and children, and other unnecessary disadvantages to dog ownership can be eliminated by simple obedience training. The elementary exercises of heeling, sitting, staying and lying down can keep the dog out of trouble in most situations.

The only tools needed for basic obedience training are a slip collar made of chain link, leather or nylon and a strong six-foot leather leash with a good spring snap. Reviewing the requirements and basic techniques given earlier, let's proceed with the dog's schooling.

Heeling. Keep your dog on your left side, with the leash in your left hand. Start straight ahead in a brisk walk. If your dog pulls ahead, jerk (do not pull) the leash and say "Heel" firmly. If the dog persists in pulling ahead, stop, turn right or left and go on for several yards, saying "Heel" each time you change direction.

If your dog balks, fix leash *under* his throat and coax him forward by repeating his name and tapping your hip.

Whatever you do, don't stop walking! If the dog jumps up or "fights" the leash, just keep moving briskly. Sooner than later he will catch on and with the repetition of "Heel" on every correction, you will have him trotting by your side with style and respect.

Sit. Keeping your dog on leash, hold his neck up and push his rump down while repeating "Sit." If he resists, "spank" him lightly several times on his rump. Be firm, but not cruel. Repeat this lesson often until it is learned perfectly. When the dog knows the command, test him at a distance without the leash. Return to him every time he fails to sit and repeat the exercise.

Stay. If you have properly trained your dog to "Sit," the "Stay" is simple. Take his leash off and repeat "Stay" holding your hand up, palm toward dog, and move away. If dog moves toward you, you must repeat the "sit" lesson until properly learned. After your

11

dog "stays" while you are in sight, move out of his sight and keep repeating "Stay." Once he has learned to "stay" even while you are out of his sight, you can test him under various conditions, such as when another dog is near, a child is playing close to him, or a car appears on the road. (Warning: do not tax your dog's patience on the "stay" until he has learned the performance perfectly.)

Down. For this lesson, keep your dog on leash. First tell him to "sit." When he has sat for a minute, place your shoe over his leash between the heel and sole. Slowly pull on the leash and repeat "Down" while you push his head down with your other hand. Do this exercise very quietly so that dog does not become excited and uncontrollable. In fact, this performance is best trained when the dog is rather quiet. Later, after the dog has learned the voice signal perfectly, you can command the "Down" with a hand signal, sweeping your hand from an upright position to a downward motion with your palm toward the dog. Be sure to say "Down" with the hand signal.

For more advanced obedience the following guides by Blanche Saunders are recommended:

The Complete Novice Obedience Course
The Complete Open Obedience Course
The Complete Utility Obedience Course (with Tracking)
Dog Training for Boys and Girls (includes simple tricks.)
All are published by Howell Book House at $3.00 each.

OBEDIENCE TRIALS

Booklets covering the rules and regulations of Obedience Trials may be obtained from The American Kennel Club, 51 Madison Avenue, New York, N.Y. 10010. In Canada, write The Canadian Kennel Club, 667 Yonge Street, Toronto, Ontario.

Both these national clubs can give you the names and locations of local and regional dog clubs that conduct training classes in obedience and run Obedience Trials in which trained dogs compete for degrees as follow: CD (Companion Dog), CDX (Companion Dog Excellent), UD (Utility Dog), TD (Tracking Dog) and UDT (Utility Dog, Tracking.)

The Exhibition of Dogs

NOBODY should exhibit a dog in the shows unless he can win without gloating and can lose without rancor. The showing of dogs is first of all a sport, and it is to be approached in a sportsmanlike spirit. It is not always so approached. That there are so many wretched losers and so many supercilious winners among the exhibitors in dog shows is the reason for this warning.

The confidence that one's dog is of exhibition excellence is all that prompts one to enter him in the show, but, if he fails in comparison with his competitors, nobody is harmed. It is no personal disgrace to have a dog beaten. It may be due to the dog's fundamental faults, to its condition, or to inexpert handling. One way to avoid such hazards is to turn the dog over to a good professional handler. Such a man with a flourishing established business will not accept an inferior dog, one that is not worth exhibiting. He will put the dog in the best possible condition before he goes into the ring with him, and he knows all the tricks of getting out of a dog all he has to give. Good handlers come high, however. Fees for taking a dog into the ring will range from ten to twenty-five dollars, plus any cash prizes the dog may win, and plus a bonus for wins made in the group.

Handlers do not win all the prizes, despite the gossip that they do, but good handlers choose only good dogs and they usually finish at or near the top of their classes. It is a mistake to assume that this is due to any favoritism or any connivance with the judges; the handlers have simply chosen the best dogs, conditioned them well, and so maneuvered them in the ring as to bring out their best points.

The services of a professional handler are not essential, however. Many an amateur shows his dogs as well, but the exhibitor without previous experience is ordinarily at something of a disadvantage. If the dog is good enough, he may be expected to win.

The premium list of the show, setting forth the prizes to be offered, giving the names of the judges, containing the entry form, and describing the conditions under which the show is to be held, are usually mailed out to prospective exhibitors about a month before the show is scheduled to be held. Any show superintendent is glad to add names of interested persons to the mailing list.

Entries for a Licensed show close at a stated date, usually about two weeks before the show opens, and under the rules no entry may be accepted after the advertised date of closing. It behooves the exhibitor to make his entries promptly. The exhibitor is responsible for all errors he may make on the entry form of his dog; such errors cannot be rectified and may result in the disqualification of the exhibit. It therefore is wise for the owner to double check all data submitted with an entry. The cost of making an entry, which is stated in the premium list, is usually from six to eight dollars. An unregistered dog may be shown at three shows, after which he must be registered or a statement must be made to the American Kennel Club that he is ineligible for registry and why, with a request for permission to continue to exhibit the dog. Such permission is seldom denied. The listing fee for an unregistered dog is twenty-five cents, which must be added to the entry fee.

Match or Sanctioned shows are excellent training and experience for regular bench shows. Entry fees are low, usually ranging from fifty cents to a dollar, and are made at the show instead of in advance. Sanctioned shows are unbenched, informal affairs where the puppy may follow his owner about on the leash and become accustomed to strange dogs, to behaving himself in the ring, and to being handled by a judge. For the novice exhibitor, too, Sanctioned shows will provide valuable experience, for ring procedure is similar to that at regular bench shows.

The classes open at most shows and usually divided by sex are as follows: Puppy Class (often Junior Puppy for dogs 6 to 9 months old, and Senior Puppy for dogs 9 to 12 months); Novice Class, for dogs that have never won first in any except the Puppy Class; Bred-by-Exhibitor Class, for dogs of which the breeder and owner are the same person or persons; the American-bred Class, for dogs whose parents were mated in America; and the Open Class, which is open to all comers. The respective first prize winners of these various classes compete in what is known as the Winners Class for points toward championship. No entry can be made in the Winners Class, which is open without additional charge to the winners of the earlier classes, all of which are obligated to compete.

A dog eligible to more than one class can be entered in each of them, but it is usually wiser to enter him in only one. A puppy should, unless unusually precocious and mature, be placed in the Puppy Class, and it is unfair to so young a dog to expect him to defeat older dogs, although an exceptional puppy may receive an award in the Winners Class. The exhibitor who is satisfied merely that his dog may win the class in which he is entered is advised to place him in the lowest class to which he is eligible, but the exhibitor with confidence in his dog and shooting for high honors should enter the dog in the Open Class, where the competition is usually the toughest. The winner of the Open Class usually (but by no means always) is also the top of the Winners Class; the runner-up to this dog is named Reserve Winners.

The winner of the Winners Class for dogs competes with the Winners Bitch for Best of Winners, after competing for Best of Breed or Best of Variety with any Champions of Record which may be entered for Specials Only. In the closing hours of the show, the Best of Breed or Best of Variety is eligible to compete in the respective Variety Group to which his breed belongs. And if, perchance, he should win his Variety Group, he is obligated to compete for Best Dog in Show. This is a major honor which few inexperienced exhibitors attain and to which they seldom aspire.

Duly entered, the dog should be brought into the best possible condition for his exhibition in the show and taught to move and to pose at his best. He should be equipped with a neat, strong collar without ornaments or spikes, a show lead of the proper length, width and material for his size and coat, and a nickel bench chain

15

of strong links with which to fasten him to his bench. Food such as the dog is used to, a bottle of the water he is accustomed to drink, and all grooming equipment should be assembled in a bag the night before departure for the show. The exhibitor's pass, on which the dog is assigned a stall number, is sent by mail by the show superintendent and should not be left behind, since it is difficult to have the pass duplicated and it enables the dog's caretaker to leave and return to the show at will.

The time of the opening of the show is stated in the premium list, and it is wise to have one's dog at the show promptly. Late arrivals are subject to disqualification if they are protested.

Sometimes examination is made by the veterinarian at the entrance of the show, and healthy dogs are quickly passed along. Once admitted to the show, if it is a "benched" show, it is wise to find one's bench, the number of which is on the exhibitor's ticket, to affix one's dog to the bench, and not to remove him from it except for exercising or until he is to be taken into the ring to be judged. A familiar blanket or cushion for the bench makes a dog feel at home there. It is contrary to the rules to remove dogs from their benches and to keep them in crates during show hours, and these rules are strictly enforced. Many outdoor shows are not "benched," and you provide your own crate or place for your dog.

At bench shows some exhibitors choose to sit by their dog's bench, but if he is securely chained he is likely to be safe in his owner's absence. Dogs have been stolen from their benches and others allegedly poisoned in the shows, but such incidents are rare indeed. The greater danger is that the dog may grow nervous and insecure, and it is best that the owner return now and again to the bench to reassure the dog of his security.

The advertised program of the show permits exhibitors to know the approximate hour of the judging of their respective breeds. Although that time may be somewhat delayed, it may be depended upon that judging will not begin before the stated hour. The dog should have been groomed and made ready for his appearance in the show ring. When his class is called the dog should be taken unhurriedly to the entrance of the ring, where the handler will receive an arm band with the dog's number.

When the class is assembled and the judge asks that the dogs be paraded before him, the handler should fall into the counter-clock-wise line and walk his dog until the signal to stop is given. In moving in a circle, the dog should be kept on the inside so that he may be readily seen by the judge, who stands in the center of the ring. In stopping the line, there is no advantage to be gained in maneuvering one's dog to the premier position, since the judge will change the position of the dogs as he sees fit.

Keep the dog alert and facing toward the judge at all times. When summoned to the center of the ring for examination, go briskly but not brashly. It is unwise to enter into conversation with the judge, except briefly to reply to any questions he may ask. Do not call his attention to any excellences the dog may possess or excuse any shortcomings; the judge is presumed to evaluate the exhibit's merits as he sees them.

If asked to move the dog, he should be led directly away from the judge and again toward the judge. A brisk but not too rapid trot is the gait the judge wishes to see, unless he declares otherwise. He may ask that the movement be repeated, with which request the handler should respond with alacrity. It is best not to choke a dog in moving him, but rather to move him on a loose lead. The judge will assign or signal a dog to his position, which should be assumed without quibble.

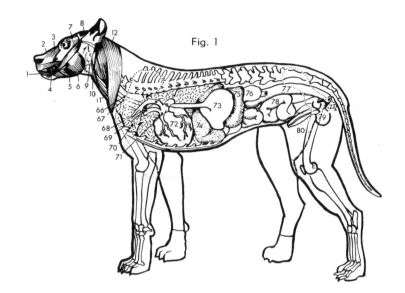

Fig. 1

Fig. 2

<table>
</table>

Fig. 1

1 Orbicularis oris.
2 Levator nasolabialis.
3 Levator labii superioris proprius (levator of upper lip).
4 Dilator naris lateralis.
5 Zygomaticus.
6 Masseter (large and well developed in the dog).
7 Scutularis.
8 Parotid Gland.
9 Submaxillary Gland.
10 Parotido-auricularis.
11 Sterno-hyoideus.
12 Brachio-cephalicus.

(Between figures 8 and 12 on top the Elevator and Depressor muscles of the ear are to be seen.)

66 Œsophagus (gullet).
67 Trachea (wind pipe).
68 Left Carotid Artery.
69 Anterior Aorta.
70 Lungs.
71 Posterior Aorta.
72 Heart.
73 Stomach.

74 Liver. (The line in front of Liver shows the Diaphragm separating Thoracic from Abdominal cavity.)
75 Spleen.
76 Kidney (left).
77 Rectum.
77A Anal Glands (position) just inside rectum.
78 Intestine.
79 Testicle.
80 Penis.
(Midway between 76 and 79 is the seat of the Bladder and behind this the seat of the Prostate gland in males, uterus in females.)

Fig. 2

Section of Head and Neck.
1 Nasal septum.
2 Tongue.
3 Cerebrum.
4 Cerebellum.
5 Medulla oblongata.
6 Spinal Cord.
7 Œsophagus (gullet).
8 Trachea (wind pipe).
9 Hard palate.
10 Soft palate.
11 Larynx, containing vocal cords.

18

The Feeding of Dogs, Constitutional Vigor

IN selecting a new dog, it is quite as essential that he shall be of sound constitution as that he shall be of the correct type of his own particular breed. The animal that is thoroughly typical of his breed is likely to be vigorous, with a will and a body to surmount diseases and ill treatment, but the converse of this statement is not always true. A dog may have constitutional vigor without breed type. We want both.

Half of the care and effort of rearing a dog is saved by choosing at the outset a puppy of sound constitution, one with a will and an ability to survive and flourish in spite of such adversity and neglect as he may encounter in life. This does not mean that the reader has any intention of obtaining a healthy dog and ill treating it, trusting its good constitution to bring it through whatever crises may beset it. It only means that he will save himself work, expense, and disappointment if only he will exercise care in the first place to obtain a healthy dog, one bred from sound and vigorous parents and one which has received adequate care and good food.

The first warning is not to economize too much in buying a dog. Never accept a cull of the litter at any price. The difference in first cost between a fragile, ill nourished, weedy, and unhealthy puppy and a sound, vigorous one, with adequate substance and the will to survive, may be ten dollars or it may be fifty dollars. But whatever it may be, it is worthwhile. A dog is an investment and it

19

is not the cost but the upkeep that makes the difference. We may save fifty dollars on the first price of a dog, only to lay out twice or five times that sum for veterinary fees over and above what it would cost to rear a dog of sound fundamental constitution and structure.

The vital, desirable dog, the one that is easy to rear and worth the care bestowed upon him, is active, inquisitive, and happy. He is sleek, his eyes free from pus or tears, his coat shining and alive, his flesh adequate and firm. He is not necessarily fat, but a small amount of surplus flesh, especially in puppyhood, is not undesirable. He is free from rachitic knobs on his joints or from crooked bones resultant from rickets. His teeth are firm and white and even. His breath is sweet to the smell. Above all, he is playful and responsive. Puppies, like babies, are much given to sleep, but when they are awake the sturdy ones do not mope lethargically around.

An adult dog that is too thin may often be fattened; if he is too fat he may be reduced. But it is essential that he shall be sound and healthy with a good normal appetite and that he be active and full of the joy of being alive. He must have had the benefit of a good heredity and a good start in life.

A dog without a fundamental inheritance of good vitality, or one that has been neglected throughout his growing period is seldom worth his feed. We must face these facts at the very beginning. Buy only from an owner who is willing to guarantee the soundness of his stock, and before consummating the purchase, have the dog, whether puppy or adult, examined by a veterinarian in order to determine the state of the dog's health.

If the dog to be cared for has been already acquired, there is nothing to do but to make the best of whatever weaknesses or frailties he may possess. But, when it is decided to replace him with another, let us make sure that he has constitutional vigor.

THE FEEDING AND NUTRITION OF
THE ADULT DOG

The dog is a carnivore, an eater of meat. This is a truism that cannot be repeated too often. Dog keepers know it but are prone to disregard it, although they do so at their peril and the peril of their dogs. Despite all the old-wives' tales to the contrary, meat does not cause a dog to be vicious, it does not give him worms nor cause him to have fits. It is his food. This is by no means all that is needed to know about food for the dog, but it is the essential knowledge. Give a dog enough sound meat and he will not be ill fed.

The dog is believed to have been the first of the animals that was brought under domestication. In his feral state he was almost exclusively an eater of meat. In his long association with man, however, his metabolism has adjusted itself somewhat to the consumption of human diet until he now can eat, even if he cannot flourish upon, whatever his master chooses to share with him, be it caviar or corn pone. It is not to be denied that a mature dog can survive without ill effects upon an exclusive diet of rice for a considerable period, but it is not to be recommended that he should be forced to do so.

Even if we had no empirical evidence that dogs thrive best upon foods of animal origin, and we possess conclusive proof of that fact, the anatomy and physiology of the dog would convince us of it. An observation of the structure of the dog's alimentary canal, superimposed upon many trial and error methods of feeding, leads us to the conclusion that a diet with meat predominating is the best food we can give a dog.

To begin with, the dental formation of the dog is typical of the carnivores. His teeth are designed for tearing rather than for mastication. He bolts his food and swallows it with a minimum of chewing. It is harmless that he should do this. No digestion takes place in the dog's mouth.

The capacity of the dog's stomach is great in comparison with the size of his body and with the capacity of his intestines. The amounts of carbohydrates and of fats digested in the stomach are minimal. The chief function of the dog's stomach is the digestion of proteins. In the dog as in the other carnivores, carbohydrates

21

and fats are digested for the most part in the small intestine, and absorption of food materials is largely from the small intestine. The enzymes necessary for the completion of the digestion of proteins which have not been fully digested in the stomach and for the digestion of sugars, starches, and fats are present in the pancreatic and intestinal juices. The capacity of the small intestine in the dog is not great and for that reason digestion that takes place there must be rapid.

The so-called large intestine (although in the dog it is really not "large" at all) is short and of small capacity in comparison with that of animals adapted by nature to subsist wholly or largely upon plant foods. In the dog, the large gut is designed to serve chiefly for storage of a limited and compact bulk of waste materials, which are later to be discharged as feces. Some absorption of water occurs there, but there is little if any absorption there of the products of digestion.

It will be readily seen that the short digestive tract of the dog is best adapted to a concentrated diet, which can be quickly digested and which leaves a small residue. Foods of animal origin (flesh, fish, milk, and eggs) are therefore suited to the digestive physiology of the dog because of the ease and completeness with which they are digested as compared with plant foods, which contain considerable amounts of indigestible structural material. The dog is best fed with a concentrated diet with a minimum of roughage.

This means meat. Flesh, milk, and eggs are, in effect, vegetation partly predigested. The steer or horse eats grain and herbage, from which its long digestive tract enables it to extract the food value and eliminate the indigestible material. The carnivore eats the flesh of the herbivore, thus obtaining his grain and grass in a concentrated form suitable for digestion in his short alimentary tract. Thus it is seen that meat is the ideal as a chief ingredient of the dog's ration.

Like that of all other animals, the dog's diet must be made up of proteins, carbohydrates, fats, minerals, vitamins, and water. None of these substances may be excluded if the dog is to survive. If he fails to obtain any of them from one source, it must come from another. It may be argued that before minerals were artificially supplied in the dog's diet and before we were aware of the existence of the various vitamins, we had dogs and they (some of them)

22

appeared to thrive. However, they obtained such substances in their foods, although we were not aware of it. It is very likely that few dogs obtained much more than their very minimum of requirements of the minerals and vitamins. It is known that rickets were more prevalent before we learned to supply our dogs with ample calcium, and black tongue, now almost unknown, was a common canine disease before we supplied in the dog's diet that fraction of the vitamin B complex known as nicotinic acid. There is no way for us to know how large a portion of our dogs died for want of some particular food element before we learned to supply all the necessary ones. The dogs that survived received somewhere in their diet some of all of these compounds.

PROTEIN

The various proteins are the nitrogenous part of the food. They are composed of the amino acids, singly or in combination. There are at least twenty-two of these amino acids known to the nutritional scientists, ten of which are regarded as dietary essentials, the others of which, if not supplied in the diet, can be compounded in the body, which requires an adequate supply of all twenty-two. When any one of the essential ten amino acids is withdrawn from the diet of any animal, growth ceases or is greatly retarded. Thus, a high protein content in any food is not an assurance of its food value if taken alone; it may be lacking in one or more of the essential ten amino acids. When the absent essential amino acids are added to it in sufficient quantities or included separately in the diet, the protein may be complete and fully assimilated.

Proteins, as such, are ingested and in the digestive tract are broken down into the separate amino acids of which they are composed. These amino acids have been likened to building stones, since they are taken up by the blood stream and conveyed to the various parts of the animal as they may be required, where they are deposited and re-united with other complementary amino acids again to form bone and muscles in the resumed form of protein.

To correct amino acid deficiencies in the diet, it is not necessary to add the required units in pure form. The same object may be accomplished more efficiently by employing proteins which contain the required amino acids.

Foods of animal origin—meat, fish, eggs, and milk—supply proteins of high nutritive value, both from the standpoint of digestibility and amino acid content. Gelatin is an exception to that statement, since gelatin is very incomplete.

Even foods of animal origin vary among themselves in their protein content and amino acid balance. The protein of muscle meat does not rank quite as high as that of eggs or milk. The glandular tissues—such as liver, kidneys, sweetbreads or pancreas—contain proteins of exceptionally high nutritive value, and these organs should be added to the dog's diet whenever it is possible to do so. Each pint of milk contains two-thirds of an ounce (dry weight) of particularly high class protein, in addition to minerals, vitamins, carbohydrates, and fats. (The only dietary necessity absent

24

from milk is iron.) Animal proteins have a high content of dietary-essential amino acids, which makes them very effective in supplementing many proteins of vegetable origin. The whites of eggs, while somewhat inferior to the yolks, contain excellent proteins. The lysine of milk can be destroyed by excessive heat and the growth promoting value of its protein so destroyed. Evaporated tinned milk has not been subjected to enough heat to injure its proteins.

Thus we can readily see why meat with its concentrated, balanced, and easily assimilated proteins should form the major part of dry weight of a dog's ration.

It has never been determined how much protein the dog requires in his diet. It may be assumed to vary as to the size, age, and breed of the dog under consideration; as to the individual dog, some assimilating protein better, or utilizing more of it than others; as to the activity or inactivity of the subject; and as to the amino acid content of the protein employed. When wheat protein gliadin is fed as the sole protein, three times as much of it is required as of the milk protein, lactalbumin. It has been estimated that approximately twenty to twenty-five percent of animal protein (dry weight) in a dog's diet is adequate for maintenance in good health, although no final conclusion has been reached and probably never can be.

Our purpose, however, is not to feed the dog the minimum ration with which he can survive or even the minimum ration with which he can flourish. It is rather to give him the maximum food in quantity and balance which he can digest and enjoy without developing a paunch. Who wants to live on the minimum diet necessary for adequate sustenance? We all enjoy a full belly of good food, and so do our dogs.

Roy G. Daggs found from experimentation that milk production in the dog was influenced by the different kinds of proteins fed to it. He has pointed out that relatively high protein diets stimulate lactation and that, in the bitch, animal proteins are better suited to the synthesis of milk than plant proteins. He concluded that liver was a better source of protein for lactation than eggs or round steak.

THE CARBOHYDRATES

The carbohydrates include all the starches, the sugars, and the cellulose and hemicellulose, which last two, known as fiber, are the chief constituents of wood, of the stalks and leaves of plants, and of the coverings of seeds. There remains considerable controversy as to the amount of carbohydrates required or desirable in canine nutrition. It has been shown experimentally that the dog is able to digest large quantities of cornstarch, either raw or cooked. Rice fed to mature dogs in amounts sufficient to satisfy total energy requirements has been found to be 95 percent digested. We know that the various commercial biscuits and meals which are marketed as food for dogs are well tolerated, especially if they are supplemented by the addition of fresh meat. There seems to be no reason why they should not be included in the dog's ration.

Carbohydrates are a cheap source of energy for the dog, both in their initial cost and in the work required of the organism for their metabolism. Since there exists ample evidence that the dog has no difficulty in digesting and utilizing considerable amounts of starches and sugars for the production of energy, there is no reason why they should be excluded from his diet. Some carbohydrate is necessary for the metabolism of fats. The only danger from the employment of carbohydrates is that, being cheap, they may be employed to the exclusion of proteins and other essential elements of the dog's diet. It should be noted that meat and milk contain a measure of carbohydrates as well as of proteins.

Thoroughly cooked rice or oatmeal in moderate quantities may well be used to supplement and cheapen a meat diet for a dog without harm to him, as may crushed dog biscuit or shredded wheat waste or the waste from manufacture of other cereal foods. They are not required but may be used without harm.

Sugar and candy, of which dogs are inordinately fond, used also to be *verboten*. They are an excellent source of energy—and harmless. They should be fed in only moderate quantities.

FATS

In the dog as in man, body fat is found in largest amounts under the skin, between the muscles and around the internal organs. The fat so stored serves as a reserve source of heat and energy when the caloric value of the food is insufficient, or for temporary periods when no food is eaten. The accumulation of a certain amount of fat around vital organs provides considerable protection against cold and injury.

Before fats can be carried to the body cells by means of the circulating blood, it is necessary for them to be digested in the intestines with the aid of enzymes. Fats require a longer time for digestion than carbohydrates or proteins. For this reason, they are of special importance in delaying the sensations of hunger. This property of fats is frequently referred to as "staying power."

It is easily possible for some dogs to accumulate too much fat, making them unattractive, ungainly, and vaguely uncomfortable. This should be avoided by withholding an excess of fats and carbohydrates from the diets of such dogs whenever obesity threatens them. There is greater danger, however, that dogs may through inadequacy of their diets be permitted to become too thin.

Carbohydrates can in part be transformed to fats within the animal body. The ratio between fats and carbohydrates can therefore be varied within wide limits in the dog's ration so long as the requirements for proteins, vitamins, and minerals are adequately met. Some dogs have been known to tolerate as much as forty percent of fat in their diets over prolonged periods, but so much is not to be recommended as a general practice. Perhaps fifteen to twenty percent of fat is adequate without being too much.

Fat is a heat producing food, and the amount given a dog should be stepped up in the colder parts of the year and reduced in the summer months. In a ration low in fat it is particularly important that a good source of the fat-soluble vitamins be included or that such vitamins be artificially supplied. Weight for weight, fat has more than twice the food value of the other organic food groups—carbohydrates and proteins. The use of fat tends to decrease the amount of food required to supply caloric needs. The fats offer a means of increasing or decreasing the total sum of energy in the diet with the least change in the volume of food intake.

27

It is far less important that the dog receive more than a minimum amount of fats, however, than that his ration contain an adequate amount and quality balance of proteins. Lean meat in adequate quantities will provide him with such proteins, and fats may be added to it in the form of fat meat, suet, or lard. Small quantities of dog biscuits, cooked rice, or other cereals in the diet will supply the needed carbohydrates. However, cellulose or other roughage is not required in the diet of the carnivore. It serves only to engorge the dog's colon, which is not capacious, and to increase the volume of feces, which is supererogatory.

MINERALS

At least eleven minerals are present in the normal dog, and there are probably others occurring in quantities so minute that they have not as yet been discovered. The eleven are as follows: Calcium (lime), sodium chloride (table salt), copper, iron, magnesium, manganese, phosphorus, zinc, potassium, and iodine.

Of many of these only a trace in the daily ration is required and that trace is adequately found in meat or in almost any other normal diet. There are a few that we should be at pains to add to the diet. The others we shall ignore.

Sodium chloride (salt) is present in sufficient quantities in most meats, although, more to improve the flavor of the food than to contribute to the animal's nutrition, a small amount of salt may be added to the ration. The exact amount makes no material difference, since the unutilized portions are eliminated, largely in the urine. If the brand of salt used is iodized, it will meet the iodine requirements, which are very small. Iodine deficiency in dogs is rare, but food crops and meats grown in certain areas contain little or no iodine, and it is well to be safe by using iodized salt.

Sufficient iron is usually found in meat and milk, but if the dog appears anemic or listless the trace of iron needed can be supplied with one of the iron salts—ferric sulphate, or oxide, or ferrous gluconate. Iron is utilized in the bone marrow in the synthesis of hemoglobin in the blood corpuscles. It is used over and over; when a corpuscle is worn out and is to be replaced, it surrenders its iron before being eliminated.

When more iron is ingested than can be utilized, some is stored in the liver, after which further surplus is excreted. The liver of the newborn puppy contains enough iron to supply the organism up until weaning time. No iron is present in milk, which otherwise provides a completely balanced ration.

A diet with a reasonable content of red meat, especially of liver or kidney, is likely to be adequate in respect to its iron. However, bitches in whelp require more iron than a dog on mere maintenance. It is recommended that the liver content of bitches' diets be increased for the duration of pregnancy.

Iron requires the presence of a minute trace of copper for its utilization, but there is enough copper in well nigh any diet to supply the requirements.

Calcium and phosphorous are the only minerals of which an insufficiency is a warranted source of anxiety. This statement may not be true of adult dogs not employed for breeding purposes, but it does apply to brood bitches and to growing puppies. The entire skeleton and teeth are made largely from calcium and phosphorus, and it is essential that the organism have enough of those minerals.

If additional calcium is not supplied to a bitch in her diet, her own bone structure is depleted to provide her puppies with their share of calcium. Moreover, in giving birth to her puppies or shortly afterward she is likely to go into eclampsia as a result of calcium depletion.

The situation, however, is easily avoided. The addition of a small amount of calcium phosphate diabasic to the ration precludes any possible calcium deficiency. Calcium phosphate diabasic is an inexpensive substance and quite tasteless. It may be sprinkled in or over the food, especially that given to brood bitches and puppies. It is the source of strong bones and vigorous teeth of ivory whiteness.

But it must be mentioned that calcium cannot be assimilated into the bone structure, no matter how much of it is fed or otherwise administered, except in the presence of vitamin D. That is D's function, to facilitate the absorption of calcium and phosphorus. This will be elaborated upon in the following discussion of the vitamins and their functions.

VITAMINS

Vitamins have in the past been largely described by diseases resulting from their absence. It is recognized more and more that many of the subacute symptoms of general unfitness of dogs may be attributable to an inadequate supply in the diet of one or more of these essential food factors. It is to be emphasized that vitamins are to be considered a part of the dog's food, essential to his health and well being. They are not to be considered as medication. Often the morbid conditions resultant from their absence in the diet may be remedied by the addition of the particular needed vitamin.

The requirements of vitamins, as food, not as medication, in the diet cannot be too strongly emphasized. These vitamins may be in the food itself, or they may better be added to it as a supplement to insure an adequate supply. Except for vitamin D, of which it is remotely possible (though unlikely) to supply too much, a surplus of the vitamin substances in the ration is harmless. They are somewhat expensive and we have no disposition to waste them, but if too much of them are fed they are simply eliminated with no subsequent ill effect.

It must be realized that vitamins are various substances, each of which has a separate function. It is definitely not safe to add to a dog's (or a child's) diet something out of a bottle or box indefinitely labeled "Vitamins," as is the practice of so many persons. We must know which vitamins we are giving, what purpose each is designed to serve, and the potency of the preparation of the brand of each one we are using.

Any one of the "shotgun" vitamin preparations is probably adequate if administered in large enough dosages. Such a method may be wasteful, however; to be sure of enough of one substance, the surplus of the others is wasted. It is much better to buy a product that contains an adequate amount of each of the needed vitamins and a wasteful surplus of none. Such a procedure is cheaper in the long run.

There follows a brief description of each of the various vitamins so far discovered and a statement of what purpose in the diet they are respectively intended to serve:

Vitamin A—This vitamin in some form is an absolute requisite for good health, even for enduring life itself. Symptoms of ad-

31

vanced deficiency of vitamin A in dogs are an eye disease with resulting impaired vision, inflammation of the conjunctiva or mucous membranes which line the eyelid, and injury to the mucous membranes of the body. Less easily recognized symptoms are an apparent lowered resistance to bacterial infection, especially of the upper respiratory tract, retarded growth, and loss of weight. Diseases due to vitamin A deficiency may be well established while the dog is still gaining in weight. Lack of muscular coordination and paralysis have been observed in dogs and degeneration of the nervous system. Some young dogs deprived of vitamin A become wholly or partially deaf.

The potency of vitamin A is usually calculated in International Units, of which it has been estimated that the dog requires about 35 per day for each pound of his body weight. Such parts as are not utilized are not lost, but are stored in the liver for future use in time of shortage. A dog well fortified with this particular vitamin can well go a month or more without harm with none of it in his diet. At such times he draws upon his liver for its surplus.

It is for its content of vitamins A and D that cod-liver oil (and the oils from the livers of other fish) is fed to puppies and growing children. Fish liver oils are an excellent source of vitamin A, and if a small amount of them is included in the diet no anxiety about deficiency of vitamin A need be entertained. In buying cod-liver oil, it pays to obtain the best grade. The number of International Units it contains per teaspoonful is stated on most labels. The vitamin content of cod-liver oil is impaired by exposure to heat, light, and air. It should be kept in a dark, cool place and the bottle should be firmly stopped.

Another source of vitamin A is found in carrots but it is almost impossible to get enough carrots in a dog to do him any good. It is better and easier to use a preparation known as carotene, three drops of which contains almost the vitamin A in a bushel of carrots.

Other natural sources of vitamin A are liver, kidney, heart, cheese, egg yolks, butter and milk. If these foods, or any one of them, are generously included in the adult dog's maintenance ration, all other sources of vitamin A may be dispensed with. The ration for all puppies, however, and for pregnant and lactating bitches should be copiously fortified either with fish liver oil or with tablets containing vitamin A.

32

Vitamin B. What was formerly known as a single vitamin B has now been found to be a complex of many different factors. Some of them are, in minute quantities, very important parts of the diets of any kind of animals. The various factors of this complex, each a separate vitamin, are designated by the letter B followed by an inferior number, as B_1, B_2, or B_6.

The absence or insufficiency in the diet of Vitamin B_1, otherwise known as thiamin, has been blamed for retarded growth, loss of weight, decreased fertility, loss of appetite, and impaired digestion. A prolonged shortage of B_1 may result in paralysis, the accumulation of fluid in the tissues, and finally in death, apparently from heart failure.

It is not easy to estimate just how much B_1 a dog requires per pound of body weight, since dogs as individuals vary in their needs, and the activity of an animal rapidly depletes the thiamin in his body. The feeding of 50 International Units per day per pound of body weight is probably wasteful but harmless. That is at least enough.

Thiamin is not stored in the system for any length of time and requires a daily dosage. It is destroyed in part by heat above the boiling point. It is found in yeast (especially in brewer's yeast), liver, wheat germ, milk, eggs, and in the coloring matter of vegetables. However, few dogs or persons obtain an optimum supply of B_1 from their daily diet, and it is recommended that it be supplied to the dog daily.

Brewer's yeast, either in powdered or tablet form affords a cheap and rather efficient way to supply the average daily requirements. An overdose of yeast is likely to cause gas in the dog's stomach.

Another factor of the vitamin B complex, riboflavin, affects particularly the skin and hair. Animals fed a diet in which it is deficient are prone to develop a scruffy dryness of the skin, especially about the eyes and mouth, and the hair becomes dull and dry, finally falling out, leaving the skin rough and dry. In experiments with rats deprived of riboflavin the toes have fallen off.

Riboflavin is present in minute quantities in so many foods that a serious shortage in any well balanced diet is unlikely. It is especially to be found in whey, which is the explanation of the smooth skin and lively hair of so many dogs whose ration contains cottage cheese.

33

While few dogs manifest any positive shortage of riboflavin, experiments on various animals have shown that successively more liberal amounts of it in their diets, up to about four times as much as is needed to prevent the first signs of deficiency, result in increased positive health.

Riboflavin deteriorates with exposure to heat and light. Most vitamin products contain it in ample measure.

Dogs were immediately responsible for the discovery of the existence of vitamin B_2, or nicotinic acid, formerly known as vitamin G. The canine disease of black tongue is analogous with the human disease called pellagra, both of which are prevented and cured by sufficient amounts of nicotinic acid in the diet. Black tongue is not a threat for any dog that eats a diet which contains even a reasonable quantity of lean meat, but it used to be prevalent among dogs fed exclusively upon corn bread or corn-meal mush, as many were.

No definite optimum dosage has been established. However, many cases of vaguely irritated skin, deadness of coat, and soft, spongy, or bleeding gums have been reported to be remedied by administration of nicotinic acid.

It has been demonstrated that niacin is essential if a good sound healthy appetite is to be maintained. Pantothenic acid is essential to good nerve health. Pyridoxin influences proper gastro-intestinal functions. Vitamin B_{12}, the "animal protein factor," is essential for proper growth and health in early life. And the water soluble B factor affects the production of milk.

Vitamin C, the so-called anti-scorbutic vitamin, is presumed to be synthesized by the dog in his own body. The dog is believed not to be subject to true scurvy. Vitamin C, then, can well be ignored as pertains to the dog. It is the most expensive of the vitamins, and, its presence in the vitamin mixture for the dog will probably do no good.

Vitamin D, the anti-rachitic vitamin, is necessary to promote the assimilation of calcium and phosphorus into the skeletal structure. One may feed all of those minerals one will, but without vitamin D they will pass out of the system unused. It is impossible to develop sound bones and teeth without its presence. Exposure to sunshine unimpeded by glass enables the animal to manufacture vitamin D in his system, but sunshine is not to be depended upon for an entire supply.

Vitamin D is abundant in cod-liver oil and in the liver oils of some other fish, or it may be obtained in a dry form in combination with other vitamins. One International Unit per pound of body weight per day is sufficient to protect a dog from rickets. From a teaspoonful to a tablespoonful of cod-liver oil a day will serve well instead for any dog.

This is the only one of the vitamins with which overdosage is possible and harmful. While a dog will not suffer from several times the amount stated and an excess dosage is unlikely, it is only fair to warn the reader that it is at least theoretically possible.

Vitamin E is the so-called fertility vitamin. Whether it is required for dogs has not as yet been determined. Rats fed upon a ration from which vitamin E was wholly excluded became permanently sterile, but the finding is not believed to pertain to all animals. Some dog keepers, however, declare that the feeding of wheat germ oil, the most abundant source of vitamin E, has prevented early abortions of their bitches, has resulted in larger and more vigorous litters of puppies, has increased the fertility of stud dogs, has improved the coats of their dogs and furthered the betterment of their general health. Whether vitamin E or some other factor or factors in the wheat germ oil is responsible for these alleged benefits is impossible to say.

Vitamin E is so widely found in small quantities in well nigh all foods that the hazard of its omission from any normal diet is small.

Numerous other vitamins have been discovered and isolated in recent years, and there are suspected to be still others as yet unknown. The ones here discussed are the only ones that warrant the use of care to include them in the dog's daily ration. It is well to reiterate that vitamins are not medicine, but are food, a required part of the diet. Any person interested in the complete nutrition of his dog will not neglect them.

It should go without saying that a dog should have access to clean, fresh, pure drinking water at all times, of which he should be permitted to drink as much or as little as he chooses. The demands of his system for drinking water will depend in part upon the moisture content of his food. Fed upon dry dog biscuits, he will probably drink considerable water to moisten it; with a diet which contains much milk or soup, he will need little additional water.

That he chooses to drink water immediately after a meal is harmless. The only times his water should be limited (but not entirely withheld from him) is after violent exercise or excitement, at which times his thirst should be satisfied only gradually.

The quantities of food required daily by dogs are influenced and determined by a number of factors: the age, size, individuality, and physical condition of the animal; the kind, quality, character, and proportions of the various foods in the ration; the climate, environment and methods of management; and the type and amount of work done, or the degree of exercise. Of these considerations, the age and size of the dog and the kind and amount of work are particularly important in determining food requirements. During early puppyhood a dog may require two or three (or even more) times as much food per pound of body weight as the same dog will require at maturity.

Any statement we should make here about the food requirements of a dog as to weight or volume would be subject to modification. Dogs vary in their metabolism. One dog might stay fat and sleek on a given amount of a given ration, whereas his litter brother in an adjoining kennel might require twice or only half as much of the same ration to maintain him in the same state of flesh.

The only sound determiners of how much to feed a dog are his appetite and his condition. As a general rule, a dog should have as much food for maintenance as he will readily clean up in five or ten minutes, unless he tends to lay on unwanted fat, in which case his intake of food should be reduced, especially its content of fats and carbohydrates. A thin dog should have his ration increased and be urged to eat it. The fats in his ration should be increased, and he may be fattened with a dessert of candy, sugar, or sweet cake following his main meal. These should never be used before a meal, lest they impair the appetite, and they should not be given to a fat dog at all. Rightly employed, they are useful and harmless, contrary to the prevalent belief.

Growing puppies require frequent meals, as will be discussed later. Pregnant and lactating bitches and frequently used stud dogs should have at least two meals, and better three, each day. For the mere maintenance of healthy adult dogs, one large meal a day appears to suffice as well as more smaller ones. Many tender-hearted dog keepers choose to divide the ration into two parts

36

and to feed their dogs twice each day. There can be no objection offered to such a program except that it involves additional work for the keeper. Whether one meal or two, they should be given at regular hours, to which dogs soon adjust and expect their dinner at a given time.

It is better to determine upon an adequate ration, with plenty of meat in it, and feed it day after day, than to vary the diet in the assumption that a dog tires of eating the same thing. There is no evidence that he does, and it is a burden upon his carnivorous digestion to be making constant adjustments and readjustments to a new diet.

Today there are available for dogs many brands of canned foods, some good and others not so good. But it is safe to feed your dog exclusively—if you do not object to the cost—a canned dog food which has been produced by a reliable concern. Many of the producers of canned dog foods are subject to Federal inspection because they also process meat and meat products for human consumption. The Federal regulations prohibit the use of diseased or unsuitable by-products in the preparation of dog food. Some of the canned dog foods on the market are mostly cereal. A glance at the analysis chart on the label will tell you whether a particular product is a good food for your dog.

If fish is fed, it should be boned—thoroughly. The same is true of fowl and rabbit meats. Small bones may be caught in the dog's throat or may puncture the stomach or intestines. Large, raw shank bones of beef may be given to the dog with impunity, but they should be renewed at frequent intervals before they spoil. A dog obtains much amusement from gnawing a raw bone, and some nutrition. Harm does not accrue from his swallowing of bone fragments, which are dissolved by the hydrochloric acid in his stomach. If the dog is fed an excessive amount of bones, constipation may result. When this occurs, the best way to relieve the condition is by the use of the enema bag. Medicinal purges of laxatives given at this time may cause irreparable damage.

Meat for dogs may be fed raw, or may be roasted, broiled, or boiled. It is not advisable to feed fried foods to dogs. All soups, gravies and juices from cooked meat must be conserved and included in the food, since they contain some of the minerals and vitamins extracted from the meat.

37

A well-known German physician selected a medium sized, strong, healthy bitch, and after she had been mated, he fed her on chopped horse meat from which the salts were to a large extent extracted by boiling for two hours in distilled water. In addition to this she was given each day a certain quantity of fried fat. As drink she had only distilled water. She gave birth to six healthy puppies, one of which was killed immediately, and its bones found to be strong and well built and free from abnormalities. The other puppies did not thrive, but remained weak, and could scarcely walk at the end of a month, when four died from excessive feebleness. And the sixth was killed two weeks· later. The mother in the meantime had become very lean but was tolerably lively and had a fair appetite. She was killed one hundred and twenty-six days after the beginning of the experiment, and it was then found that the bones of her spine and pelvis were softened—a condition known to physicians as osteomalacia.

The results of this experiment are highly interesting and instructive, showing clearly as they do that the nursing mother sends out to her young, in her milk, a part of her store of lime, which is absolutely essential to their welfare. They show also that if proper food is denied her, when in whelp and when nursing, not only her puppies but she as well must suffer greatly in consequence. And in the light of these facts is uncovered one of the most potential causes of rickets, so common among large breeds.

It may therefore be accepted that bitches in whelp must have goodly quantities of meat; moreover, that while cooking may be the rule if the broth is utilized, it is a wise plan to give the food occasionally in the raw state.

There is little choice among the varieties of meat, except that pork is seldom relished by dogs, usually contains too much fat, and should be cooked to improve its digestibility when it is used at all. Beef, mutton, lamb, goat, and horse flesh are equally valuable. The choice should be made upon the basis of their comparative cost and their availability in the particular community. A dog suddenly changed from another diet to horse flesh may develop a harmless and temporary diarrhea, which can be ignored. Horse flesh is likely to be deficient in fats, which may be added in the form of suet, lard or pure corn oil.

The particular cuts of whatever meat is used is of little consequence. Liver and kidney are especially valuable and when it is possible they should be included as part of the meat used. As the only meat in the ration, liver and kidney tend to loosen the bowels. It is better to include them as a part of each day's ration than to permit them to serve as the sole meat content one or two days a week.

It makes no difference whether meat is ground or is fed to the dog in large or medium sized pieces. He is able to digest pieces of meat as large as he can swallow. The advantage of grinding meat is that it can be better mixed with whatever else it is wished to include in the ration, the dog being unable to pick out the meat and reject the rest. There is little harm in his doing so, except for the waste, since it is the meat upon which we must depend for the most part for his nutrition.

Fresh ground meat can be kept four or five days under ordinary refrigeration without spoiling. It may be kept indefinitely if solidly frozen. Frozen ground horse meat for dogs is available in many markets, is low in price, and is entirely satisfactory for the purpose intended.

A suggested ration is made as follows: Two-thirds to three-quarters by weight of ground meat including ten to twenty percent of fat and a portion of liver or kidney, with the remainder thoroughly cooked rice or oatmeal, or shredded wheat, or dog biscuit, or wheat germ, with a sprinkling of calcium phosphate diabasic. Vitamins may be added, or given separately.

If it is desired to offer the dog a second meal, it may be of shredded wheat or other breakfast cereal with plenty of milk, with or without one or more soft boiled eggs. Evaporated canned milk or powdered milk is just as good food for the dog as fresh milk. Cottage cheese is excellent for this second meal.

These are not the only possible rations for the dog, but they will prove adequate. Leavings from the owner's table can be added to either ration, but can hardly be depended upon for the entire nourishment of the dog.

The dog's food should be at approximately body heat, tepid but never hot.

Little consideration is here given to the costs of the various foods. Economies in rations and feeding practices are admittedly desirable, but not if they are made at the expense of the dog's health.

SOME BRIEF PRECEPTS ABOUT FEEDING

Many dogs are overfed. Others do not receive adequate rations. Both extremes should be avoided, but particularly overfeeding of grown dogs. Coupled with lack of exercise, overfeeding usually produces excessive body weight and laziness, and it may result in illness and sterility. Prolonged undernourishment causes loss of weight, listlessness, dull coats, sickness, and death.

An adequate ration will keep most mature dogs at a uniform body weight and in a thrifty, moderately lean condition. Observation of condition is the best guide in determining the correct amount of food.

The axiom, "One man's meat is another man's poison," is applicable to dogs also. Foods that are not tolerated by the dog or those that cause digestive and other disturbances should be discontinued. The use of moldy, spoiled, or rotten food is never good practice. Food should be protected from fouling by rats or mice, especially because rats are vectors of leptospirosis. The excessive use of food of low energy content and low biological values will often result in poor condition and may cause loss of weight and paunchiness.

All feeding and drinking utensils must be kept scrupulously clean. They should be washed after each using.

It is usually desirable to reduce the food allotment somewhat during hot weather. Dogs should be fed at regular intervals, and the best results may be expected when regular feeding is accompanied by regular, but not exhausting, exercise.

Most dogs do not thrive on a ration containing large amounts of sloppy foods, and excessive bulk is to be avoided especially for hardworking dogs, puppies, and pregnant or lactating bitches. If the ration is known to be adequate and the dog is losing weight or is not in good condition, the presence of intestinal parasites is to be suspected. However, dogs sometimes go "off feed" for a day or two. This is cause for no immediate anxiety, but if it lasts more than two or three days, a veterinarian should be consulted.

FOOD FOR THE STUD DOG

The stud dog that is used for breeding only at infrequent intervals requires only the food needed for his maintenance in good health, as set forth in the foregoing pages. He should be well fed with ample meat in his diet, moderately exercised to keep his flesh firm and hard, and not permitted to become too thin or too fat.

More care is required for the adequate nutrition of the dog offered at public stud and frequently employed for breeding. A vigorous stud dog may very handily serve two bitches a week over a long period without a serious tax upon his health and strength if he is fully nourished and adequately but not excessively exercised. Such a dog should have at least two meals a day, and they should consist of even more meat, milk (canned is as good as fresh), eggs, cottage cheese, and other foods of animal origin than is used in most maintenance rations. Liver and some fat should be included, and the vitamins especially are not to be forgotten. In volume this will be only a little more than the basic maintenance diet, the difference being in its richness and concentration.

An interval of an hour or two should intervene between a dog's meal and his employment for breeding. He may be fed, but only lightly, immediately after he has been used for breeding.

The immediate reason that a stud dog should be adequately fed and exercised is the maintenance of his strength and virility. The secondary reason is that a popular stud dog is on exhibition at all times, between the shows as well as at the shows. Clients with bitches to be bred appear without notice to examine a dog at public stud, and the dog should be presented to them in the best possible condition—clean, hard, in exactly the most becoming state of flesh, and with a gleaming, lively coat. These all depend largely upon the highly nutritious diet the dog receives.

FOOD FOR THE BROOD BITCH

Often a well fed bitch comes through the ordeal of rearing a large litter of puppies without any impairment of her vitality and flesh. In such case she may be returned to a good maintenance ration until she is ready to be bred again. About the time she weans her puppies her coat will be dead and ready to drop out, but if she is healthy and well fed a new and vigorous coat will grow in, and she will be no worse off for her maternal ordeal. Some bitches, either from a deficient nutrition or a constitutional disposition to contribute too much of their own strength and substance to the nutrition of the puppies, are thin and exhausted at the time of weaning. Such a bitch needs the continuance of at least two good and especially nutritious meals a day for a month or more until her flesh and strength are restored before she is returned to her routine maintenance ration, upon which she may be kept until time comes to breed her again.

At breeding time a bitch's flesh should be hard, and she should be on the lean side rather than too fat. No change in her regular maintenance diet need be made until about the fourth or fifth week of her pregnancy. The growth of the fetus is small up until the middle of the pregnancy, after which it becomes rapid.

The bitch usually begins to "show in whelp" in four to six weeks after breeding, and her food consumption should be then gradually stepped up. If she has been having only one meal a day, she should be given two; if she has had two, both should be larger. Henceforth until her puppies are weaned, she must eat not merely for two, as is said of the pregnant woman, but for four or five, possibly for ten or twelve. She is not to be encouraged to grow fat. Especial emphasis should be laid upon her ration's content of meat, including liver, milk, calcium phosphate, and vitamins A and D, both of which are found in cod-liver oil.

Some breeders destroy all but a limited number of puppies in a litter in the belief that a bitch will be unable adequately to nourish all the puppies she has whelped. In some extreme cases it may be necessary to do this or to obtain a foster mother or wet nurse to share the burden of rearing the puppies. However, the healthy bitch with normal metabolism can usually generate enough milk to feed adequately all the puppies she has produced, provided she is well enough fed and provided the puppies are fed additionally as soon as they are able to eat.

After whelping until the puppies are weaned, throughout the lactating period, the bitch should have all the nourishing food she can be induced to eat—up to four or five meals a day. These should consist largely of meat and liver, some fat, a small amount of cereals, milk, eggs, cottage cheese, calcium phosphate, and vitamins, with especial reference to vitamins A and D. At that time it is hardly possible to feed a bitch too much or to keep her too fat. The growth of the puppies is much more rapid after they are born than was their growth in the dam's uterus, and the large amount of food needed to maintain that rapid growth must pass through the bitch and be transformed to milk, while at the same time she must maintain her own body.

THE FEEDING OF PUPPIES

If the number of puppies in a litter is small, if the mother is vigorous, healthy, and a good milker, the youngsters up until their weaning time may require no additional food over and above the milk they suck from their dam's breasts. If the puppies are numerous or if the dam's milk is deficient in quality or quantity, it is wise to begin feeding the puppies artificially as soon as they are able and willing to accept food. This is earlier than used to be realized.

It is for the sake of the puppies' vigor rather than for the sake of their ultimate size that their growth is to be promoted as rapidly as possible. Vigorous and healthy puppies attain early maturity if they are given the right amounts of the right quality of food. The ultimate size of the dog at maturity is laid down in his germ plasm, and he can be stunted or dwarfed, if at all, only at the expense of his type. If one tries to prevent the full growth of a dog by withholding from him the food he needs, one will wind up with a rachitic, cowhocked dog, one with a delicate digestive apparatus, a sterile one, one with all of these shortcomings combined, or even a dead dog.

Growth may be slowed with improper food, sometimes without serious harm, but the dog is in all ways better off if he is forced along with the best food and encouraged to attain his full size at an early age. Dogs of the smaller breeds usually reach their full maturity several months earlier than those of the larger breeds. A well grown dog reaches his sexual maturity and can be safely used for limited breeding at one year of age.

As soon as teeth can be felt with the finger in a puppy's mouth, which is usually at about seventeen or eighteen days of age, it is safe to begin to feed him. His first food (except for his mother's milk) should be of scraped raw beef at body temperature. The first day he may have ¼ to 2 teaspoonfuls, according to size. He will not need to learn to eat this meat; he will seize upon it avidly and lick his chops for more. The second day he may have ⅓ to 3 teaspoonfuls, according to size, with two feedings 12 hours apart. Thereafter, the amount and frequency of this feeding may be rapidly increased. By the twenty-fifth day the meat need not be scraped, but only finely ground. This process of the early feeding of raw meat to puppies not only gives them a good start in life, but

44

it also relieves their mother of a part of her burden of providing milk for them.

At about the fourth week, some cereal (thoroughly cooked oatmeal, shredded wheat, or dried bread) may be either moistened and mixed with the meat or be served to the puppies with milk, fresh or canned. It may be necessary to immerse their noses into such a mixture to teach them to eat it. Calcium phosphate and a small amount of cod-liver oil should be added to such a mixture, both of which substances the puppies should have every day until their maturity. At the fourth week, while they are still at the dam's breast, they may be fed three or four times a day upon this extra ration, or something similar, such as cottage cheese or soft boiled egg. By the sixth week their dam will be trying to wean them, and they may have four or five meals daily. One of these may be finely broken dog biscuit thoroughly soaked in milk. One or two of the meals should consist largely or entirely of meat with liver.

The old advice about feeding puppies "little and often" should be altered to "much and often." Each puppy at each meal should have all the food he will readily clean up. Food should not be left in front of the puppies. They should be fed and after two or three minutes the receptacle should be taken away. Young puppies should be roly-poly fat, and kept so up to at least five or six months of age. Thereafter they should be slightly on the fat side, but not pudgy, until maturity.

The varied diet of six-week-old puppies may be continued, but at eight or nine weeks the number of meals may be reduced to four, and at three months, to three large rations per day. After six months the meals may be safely reduced again to two a day, but they must be generous meals with meat, liver, milk, cod-liver oil, and calcium phosphate. At full maturity, one meal a day suffices, or two may be continued.

The secret of turning good puppies into fine, vigorous dogs is to keep them growing through the entire period of their maturation. The most important item in the rearing of puppies is adequate and frequent meals of highly nourishing foods. Growth requires two or three times as much food as maintenance. Time between meals should be allowed for digestion, but puppies should never be permitted to become really hungry. Water in a shallow dish should be available to puppies at all times after they are able to walk.

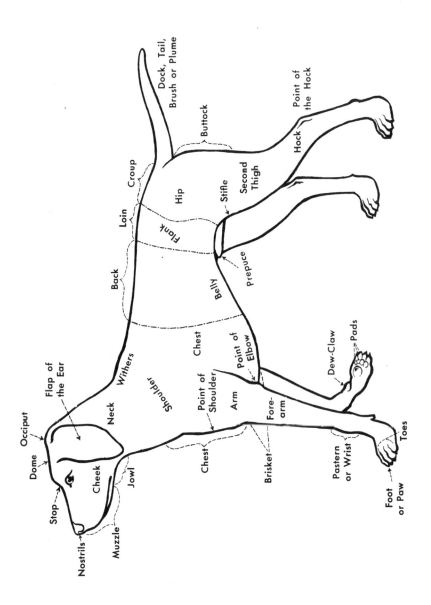

Dock, Tail, Brush or Plume

Point of the Hock

Buttock

Hock

Croup

Hip

Stifle

Second Thigh

Loin

Flank

Back

Prepuce

Belly

Chest

Point of Elbow

Arm

Pads

Withers

Shoulder

Dew-Claw

Flap of the Ear

Neck

Point of Shoulder

Fore-arm

Occiput

Chest

Dome

Cheek

Jowl

Brisket

Pastern or Wrist

Toes

Stop

Muzzle

Nostrils

Foot or Paw

46

The Breeding
of Dogs

HERE, if anywhere in the entire process of the care
and management of dogs, the exercise of good judgment is involved.
Upon the choice of the two dogs, male and female, to be mated
together depends the future success or failure of one's dogs. If the
two to be mated are ill chosen, either individually or as pertains
to their fitness as mates, one to the other, all the painstaking care
to feed and rear the resultant puppies correctly is wasted. The
mating together of two dogs is the drafting of the blueprints and
the writing of the specifications of what the puppies are to be
like. The plans, it is true, require to be executed; the puppies,
when they arrive, must be adequately fed and cared for in order
to develop them into the kinds of dogs they are in their germ plasm
designed to become. However, if the plans as determined in the
mating are defective, just so will the puppies that result from them
be defective, in spite of all the good raising one can give them.

The element of luck in the breeding of dogs cannot be discounted,
for it exists. The mating which on paper appears to be the best
possible may result in puppies that are poor and untypical of
their breed. Even less frequently, a good puppy may result from
a chance mating together of two ill chosen parents. These results
are fortuitous and unusual, however. The best dogs as a lot come
from parents carefully chosen as to their individual excellences and
as to their suitability as mates for each other. It is as unwise as

47

it is unnecessary to trust to luck in the breeding of dogs. Careful planning pays off in the long run, and few truly excellent dogs are produced without it.

Some breeders without any knowledge of genetics have been successful, without knowing exactly why they succeeded. Some of them have adhered to beliefs in old wives' tales and to traditional concepts that science has long since exploded and abandoned. Such as have succeeded have done so in spite of their lack of knowledge and not because of it.

There is insufficient space at our disposal in this book to discuss in detail the science of genetics and the application of that science to the breeding of dogs. Whole books have been written about the subject. One of the best, clearest, and easiest for the layman to understand is *The New Art of Breeding Better Dogs,* by Philip Onstott, which may be obtained from Howell Book House, the publisher. In it and in other books upon the subject of genetics will be found more data about the practical application of science to the breeding of livestock than can be included here.

The most that can be done here is to offer some advice soundly based upon the genetic laws. Every feature a dog may or can possess is determined by the genes carried in the two reproductive cells, one from each parent, from the union of which he was developed. There are thousands of pairs of these determiners in the life plan of every puppy, and often a complex of many genes is required to produce a single recognizable attribute of the dog.

These genes function in pairs, one member of each pair being contributed by the father and the other member of the pair coming from the mother. The parents obtained these genes they hand on from their parents, and it is merely fortuitous which half of any pair of genes present in a dog's or a bitch's germ plasm may be passed on to any one of the progeny. Of any pair of its own genes, a dog or a bitch may contribute one member to one puppy and the other member to another puppy in the same litter or in different litters. The unknown number of pairs of genes is so great that there is an infinite number of combinations of them, which accounts for the differences we find between two full brothers or two full sisters. In fact, it depends upon the genes received whether a dog be a male or a female.

We know that the male dog contributes one and the bitch the

48

other of every pair of genes that unite to determine what the puppy will be like and what he will grow into. Thus, the parents make exactly equal contributions to the germ plasm or zygote from which every puppy is developed. It was long believed that the male dog was so much more important than the bitch in any mating that the excellence or shortcomings of the bitch might be disregarded. This theory was subsequently reversed and breeders considered the bitch to be more important than the dog. We now know that their contribution in every mating and in every individual puppy is exactly equal, and neither is to be considered more than the other.

There are two kinds of genes—the recessive genes and the dominant. And there are three kinds of pairs of genes: a recessive from the sire plus a recessive from the dam; a dominant from the sire plus a dominant from the dam; and a dominant from one parent plus a recessive from the other. It is the last combination that is the source of our trouble in breeding. When both members of a pair of genes are recessive, the result is a recessive attribute in the animal that carries them; when both members of the pair are dominant, the result is a pure dominant attribute; but when one member of the pair is recessive and the other member dominant, the result will be a wholly or only partially dominant attribute, which will breed true only half of the time. This explains why a dog or a bitch may fail to produce progeny that looks at all like itself.

If all the pairs of a dog's genes were purely dominant, we could expect him to produce puppies that resembled himself in all particulars, no matter what kind of mate he was bred to. Or if all his genes were recessive and he were mated to a bitch with all recessive genes, the puppies might be expected to look quite like the parents. However, a dog with mixed pairs of genes bred to a bitch with mixed pairs of genes may produce anything at all, puppies that bear no resemblance to either parent.

Long before the Mendelian laws were discovered, some dogs were known to be "prepotent" to produce certain characters, that is the characters would show up in their puppies irrespective of what their mates might be like. For instance, some dogs, themselves with dark eyes, might be depended upon never to produce a puppy with light eyes, no matter how light eyed the mate to which he was bred. This was true despite the fact that the dog's litter brother which had equally dark eyes, when bred to a light eyed bitch might produce a large percentage of puppies with light eyes.

Before it is decided to breed a bitch, it is well to consider whether she is worth breeding, whether she is good enough as an individual and whether she came from a good enough family to warrant the expectations that she will produce puppies worth the expense and trouble of raising. It is to be remembered that the bitch contributes exactly half the genes to each of her puppies; if she has not good genes to contribute, the time and money involved in breeding her and rearing her puppies will be wasted.

It is conceded that a bad or mediocre bitch when bred to an excellent dog will probably produce puppies better than herself. But while one is "grading up" from mediocre stock, other breeders are also grading upward from better stock and they will keep just so far ahead of one's efforts that one can never catch up with them. A merely pretty good bitch is no good at all for breeding. It is better to dispose of a mediocre bitch or to relegate her to the position of a family pet than to breed from her. It is difficult enough, with all the care and judgment one is able to muster, to obtain superlative puppies even from a fine bitch, without cluttering the earth with inferior puppies from just any old bitch.

If one will go into the market and buy the best possible bitch from the best possible family one's purse can afford and breed her sensibly to the best and most suitable stud dog one can find, success is reasonably sure. Even if for economy's sake, the bitch is but a promising puppy backed up by the best possible pedigree, it will require only a few months until she is old enough to be bred. From such a bitch, one may expect first-rate puppies at the first try, whereas in starting with an inferior bitch one is merely lucky if in two or three generations he obtains a semblance of the kind of dog he is trying to produce.

Assuming it is decided that the bitch is adequate to serve as a brood bitch, it becomes necessary to choose for her a mate in collaboration with which she may realize the ultimate of her possibilities. It is never wise to utilize for stud the family pet or the neighbor's pet just because he happens to be registered in the studbook or because his service costs nothing. Any dog short of the best and most suitable (wherever he may be and whoever may own him) is an extravagance. If the bitch is worth breeding at all, she is worth shipping clear across the continent, if need be, to obtain for her a mate to enable her to realize her possibilities. Stud fees may range from fifty to one hundred dollars or even more. The average value of each puppy, if well reared, should at the time of weaning approximate the legitimate stud fee of its sire. With a good bitch it is therefore profitable to lay out as much as may be required to obtain the services of the best and most suitable stud dog—always assuming that he is worth the price asked. However, it is never wise to choose an inferior or unsuitable dog just because he is well ballyhooed and commands an exorbitant stud fee.

There are three considerations by which to evaluate the merits of a stud dog—his outstanding excellence as an individual, his pedigree and the family from which he derived, and the excellence or inferiority of the progeny he is known to have produced.

As an individual a good stud dog may be expected to be bold and aggressive (not vicious) and structurally typical of his breed, but without any freakish exaggerations of type. He must be sound, a free and true mover, possess fineness and quality, and be a gentleman of his own breed. Accidentally acquired scars or injuries such as broken legs should not be held against him, because he can transmit only his genes to his puppies and no such accidents impair his genes.

A dog's pedigree may mean much or little. One of two litter brothers, with pedigrees exactly alike, may prove to be a superlative show and stud dog, and the other worth exactly nothing for either purpose. The pedigree especially is not to be judged on its length, since three generations is at most all that is required, although further extension of the pedigree may prove interesting to a curious owner. No matter how well-bred his pedigree may show a dog to be, if he is not a good dog the ink required to write the pedigree was wasted.

The chief value of a pedigree is to enable us to know from which of a dog's parents, grandparents, or great-grandparents, he derived his merits, and from which his faults. In choosing a mate for him (or for her, as the case may be) one seeks to reinforce the one and to avoid the other. Let us assume that one of the grandmothers was upright in shoulder, whereas the shoulder should be well laid back; we can avoid as a mate for such a dog one with any tendency to straight shoulders or one from straight shouldered ancestry. The same principle would apply to an uneven mouth, a light eye, a soft back, splayed feet, cowhocks, or to any other inherited fault. Suppose, on the other hand, that the dog himself, the parents, and all the grandparents are particularly nice in regard to their fronts; in a mate for such a dog, one desires as good a front as is obtainable, but if she, or some of her ancestors are not too good in respect to their fronts, one may take a chance anyway and trust to the good fronted dog with his good fronted ancestry to correct the fault. That then is the purpose of the pedigree as a guide to breeding.

A stud dog can best be judged, however, by the excellence of the progeny he is known to have produced, if it is possible to obtain all the data to enable the breeder to evaluate that record. A complete comparative evaluation is perhaps impossible to make, but one close enough to justify conclusions is available. Not only the number but the quality of the bitches to which the dog has been bred must enter into the consideration. A young dog may not have had the opportunity to prove his prowess in the stud. He may have been bred to few bitches and those few of indifferent merits, or his get may not be old enough as yet to hit the shows and establish a record for themselves or for their sire. Allowance may be made for such a dog.

On the other hand, a dog may have proved himself to be phenomenal in the show ring, or may have been made to seem phenomenal by means of the owner's ballyhoo and exploitation. Half of the top bitches in the entire country may have been bred to him upon the strength of his winning record. Merely from the laws of probability such a dog, if he is not too bad, will produce some creditable progeny. It is necessary to take into consideration the opportunities a dog has had in relation to the fine progeny he has produced.

That, however, is the chief criterion by which a good stud dog may be recognized. A dog which can sire two or three excellent puppies in every litter from a reasonably good bitch may be considered as an acceptable stud. If he has in his lifetime sired one or two champions each year, and especially if one or two of the lot are superlative champions, top members of their breed, he is a great stud dog. Ordinarily and without other considerations, such a dog is to be preferred to one of his unproved sons, even though the son be as good or better an individual. In this way one employs genes one knows to produce what one wants. The son may be only hybrid dominant for his excellent qualities.

In the choice of a stud dog no attention whatever need be paid to claims that he sires numerically big litters. Unless the sire is deficient in sperm, the number of puppies in the litter, provided there are any puppies at all, depends entirely upon the bitch. At one service, a dog deposits enough spermatozoa to produce a million puppies, if there were so many ova to be fertilized. In any event, the major purpose should be to obtain good puppies, not large numbers of them.

There are three methods of breeding employed by experienced breeders—outcrossing, inbreeding, and line breeding. By outcrossing is meant the breeding together of mates of which no blood relationship can be traced. It is much favored by novice breeders, who feel that the breeding together of blood relatives is likely to result in imbecility, constitutional weakness, or some other kind of degeneration. Inbreeding is the mating together of closely related animals—father to daughter, mother to son, brother to sister, half brother to half sister. Some of the best animals ever produced have been bred from some such incestuous mating, and the danger from such practices, if they are carried out by persons who know what they are about, is minimal. Line breeding is the mating together of animals related one to another, but less closely—such as first cousins, grandsire to granddaughter, granddam to grandson, uncle to niece, or aunt to nephew.

Absolute outcrossing is usually impossible, since all the good dogs in any breed are more or less related—descended from some common ancestor in the fifth or sixth or seventh generation of their pedigrees. In any event, it is seldom to be recommended, since the results from it in the first generation of progeny are usually not satisfactory. It may be undertaken by some far-sighted and experienced breeder for the purpose of bringing into his strain some particular merit lacking in it and present in the strain of the unrelated dog. While dogs so bred may obtain an added vigor from what is known in genetics as *heterosis,* they are likely to manifest a coarseness and a lack of uniformity in the litter which is not to be found in more closely bred puppies. Good breeders never outcross if it is possible to obtain the virtues they want by sticking to their own strain. And when they do outcross, it is for the purpose of utilizing the outcrossed product for further breeding. It is not an end in itself.

Inbreeding (or incest breeding, as it is sometimes called) involves no such hazards as are and in the past have been attributed to it. It produces some very excellent dogs when correctly employed, some very bad ones even when correctly employed, and all bad ones when carelessly used. All the standard breeds of dogs were established as uniform breeds through intense inbreeding and culling over many generations. Inbreeding brings into manifestation undesirable recessive genes, the bearers of which can be discarded and the strain can thus be purged of its bad recessives.

Dogs of great soundness and excellence, from excellent parents and grandparents, all of them much alike, may be safely mated together, no matter how closely they may be related, with reasonable hope that most of the progeny will be sound and typical with a close resemblance to all the members of their ancestry. However, two such superlative and well-bred dogs are seldom to be found. It is the way to make progress rapidly and to establish a strain of dogs much alike and which breeds true. The amateur with the boldness and courage to try such a mating in the belief that his dogs are good enough for it is not to be discouraged. But if his judgment is not justified by the results, let him not complain that he has not been warned.

Line breeding is the safest course between the Scylla of outcrossing and the Charybdis of inbreeding for the inexperienced navigator in the sea of breeding. It, too, is to be used with care, because when it succeeds it partakes much of the nature of inbreeding. At any rate, its purpose is the pairing of like genes.

Here the pedigrees come into use. We examine the pedigree of the bitch to be bred. We hope that all the dogs named in it are magnificent dogs, but we look them over and choose the best of the four grandparents. We check this grandparent's breeding and find it good, as it probably is if it is itself a dog or bitch of great excellence. We shall assume that this best dog in the bitch's pedigree is the maternal grandsire. Then our bitch may be bred back to this particular grandsire, to his full brother if he has one of equal excellence, to his best son or best grandson. In such a fashion we compound the genes of this grandsire, and hope to obtain some puppies with his excellences intensified.

The best name in the pedigree may be some other dog or bitch, in which case it is his or her germ plasm that is to be doubled to serve for the foundation of the pedigrees of the puppies of the projected litter.

In making a mating, it is never wise to employ two dogs with the same positive fault. It is wise to use two dogs with as many of the same positive virtues as it is possible to obtain. Neither should faults balance each other, as one with a front too wide, the other with a front too narrow; one with a sway back, the other roach backed. Rather, one member of the mating should be right where the other is wrong. We cannot trust to obtain the intermediate, if we overcompensate the fault of one mate with a fault of the other.

NEGOTIATIONS TO USE THE STUD DOG

Plans to use a stud dog should be laid far enough in advance to enable one to make sure that the services of the dog will be available when they are required. Most men with a dog at public stud publish "stud cards," on which are printed the dog's pedigree and pertinent data pertaining to its record. These should be requested for all the dogs one contemplates using. Most such owners reserve the right to refuse to breed their dogs to bitches they deem unsuitable for them; they wish to safeguard their dog's reputation as a producer of superior puppies, by choosing the bitches to which he shall be bred. Therefore, it is advisable to submit a description of the bitch, with or without a picture of her, and her pedigree to the stud dog's owner at the time the application to use him is made.

Notification should be sent to the owner of the dog as soon as the bitch begins to show in heat, and she should be taken or sent by air or by railway express to the dog's owner about the time she is first recognized to be in full heat and ready to breed. The stud dog's owner should be advised by telegram or telephone just how she has been sent and just when she may be expected, and instruction should be given about how she is to be returned.

Extreme care should be used in securely crating a bitch for shipment when she is in heat. Such bitches are prone to chew their way out of insecure boxes and escape to be bred by some vagrant mongrel. A card containing a statement of the bitch's condition should be attached to the crate as a warning to the carrier to assure her greater security.

MATING

The only time the bitch may become pregnant is during her period of oestruation, a time also variously referred to as the "oestrus," "the season," and as being in "heat." A bitch's first season usually occurs when she is between six and nine months of age, with the average age being eight months. In rare instances it may occur as early as five months or as late as thirteen months of age. After the first season, oestrus usually recurs at intervals of approximately six months, though this too is subject to variation. Also, the bitch's cycle may be influenced by factors such as a change of environment or a change of climate, and her cycle will, of course, be changed if it is interrupted by pregnancy. Most bitches again come in season four to six months after whelping.

There is a decided controversy among breeders as to the wisdom of breeding a bitch during her first season. Some believe a really fine bitch should be bred during her first season in order that she may produce as many puppies as possible during the fertile years of her life span. Others feel that definite physical harm results from breeding a bitch at her first season. Since a normal healthy bitch can safely produce puppies until she is about nine years old, she can comfortably yield eight to ten litters with rests between them in her life. Any breeder should be satisfied with this production from one animal. It seems wiser, therefore, to avoid the risk of any harm and pass her first season. Bitches vary in temperament and in the ages at which they reach sufficient maturity for motherhood and its responsibilities. As with the human animal, stability comes with age and a dam is much more likely to be a good mother if she is out of the puppy phase herself. If the bitch is of show quality, she might become a champion between her first and second heats if not bred.

Usually, oestruation continues for a period of approximately three weeks, but this too is subject to variation. Prior to the beginning of the oestrus, there may be changes in the bitch's actions and demeanor; she may appear restless, or she may become increasingly affectionate. Often there is increased frequency of urination and the bitch may be inclined to lick her external parts. The breeder should be alert for any signs of the approach of oestrus since the bitch must be confined and protected at this time in order to preclude the possibility of the occurrence of a mating with any but the selected stud.

The first physical sign of oestrus is a bloody discharge of watery consistency. The mucous membrane lining the vulva becomes congested, enlarged, and reddened, and the external parts become puffy and swollen. The color of the discharge gradually deepens during the first day or two until it is a rich red color; then it gradually becomes lighter until by the tenth to twelfth day it has only a slightly reddish, or straw-colored, tinge. During the next day or so it becomes almost clear. During this same period, the swelling and hardness of the external parts gradually subside, and by the time the discharge has lost most of its color, the parts are softened and spongy. It is at this time that ovulation, the production of ripened ova (or eggs), takes place, although physical manifestations of oestrus may continue for another week.

A normal bitch has two ovaries which contain her ova. All the eggs she will produce during her lifetime are present in the ovaries at birth. Ordinarily, some of the ova ripen each time the bitch comes in season. Should a bitch fail to ovulate (produce ripened ova), she cannot, of course, become pregnant. Actually, only one ovary is necessary for ovulation, and loss of or damage to one ovary without impairment of the other will not prevent the bitch from producing puppies.

If fertilization does not occur, the ova (and this is also true of the sperm of the male) live only a short time—probably a couple of days at the most. Therefore, if mating takes place too long before or after ovulation, a bitch will not conceive, and the unfertilized ova will pass through the uterus into the vagina. Eventually they will either be absorbed or will pass out through the vulva by the same opening through which urination takes place. If fertilization does occur, the fertilized eggs become implanted on the inner surface of the uterus and grow to maturity.

Obviously, the breeder must exercise great care in determining when the dog and the bitch should be put together. Because the length of time between the beginning of the oestrus and the time of ovulation varies in different bitches, no hard and fast rule can be established, although the twelfth to fourteenth day is in most cases the correct time. The wise breeder will keep a daily record of the changes in the bitch's condition and will arrange to put the bitch and dog together when the discharge has become almost clear and the external parts are softened and spongy. If the bitch refuses the advances of the dog, it is preferable to separate the two, wait a day, then again permit the dog to approach the bitch.

Ordinarily, if the bitch is willing to accept the dog, fertilization of the ovum will take place. Usually one good service is sufficient, although two at intervals of twenty-four to forty-eight hours are often allowed.

Male dogs have glands on the penis which swell after passing the sphincter muscle of the vagina and "tie" the two animals together. The time may last for a period of a few minutes, a half hour, or occasionally up to an hour or more, but will end naturally when the locking glands have deflated the needful amount. While tying may increase the probability of success, in many cases no tie occurs, yet the bitches become pregnant.

Sperm are produced in the dog's testicles and are stored in the epididymis, a twisting tube at the side of the testicle. The occasional male dog whose testicles are not descended (a cryptorchid) is generally conceded to be sterile, although in a few instances it has been asserted that cryptorchids were capable of begetting progeny. The sterility in cryptorchids is believed to be due to the fact that the sperm are destroyed if the testicle remains within the abdominal cavity because the temperature is much higher there than in the normally descended testicle. Thus all sperm produced by the dog may be destroyed if both testicles are undescended. A monorchid (a dog with one testicle descended, the other undescended) may be fertile. Nevertheless, it is unwise to use a monorchid for stud purposes, because monorchidism is believed to be a heritable trait, and the monorchid, as well as the cryptorchid, is ineligible for the show ring.

After breeding, a bitch should be confined for a week to ten days to avoid mismating with another dog.

WHELPING CALENDAR

Find the month and date on which your bitch was bred in one of the left-hand columns. Directly opposite that date, in the right-hand column, is her expected date of whelping, bearing in mind that 61 days is as common as 63.

Date bred January	Date due to whelp March	Date bred February	Date due to whelp April	Date bred March	Date due to whelp May	Date bred April	Date due to whelp June	Date bred May	Date due to whelp July	Date bred June	Date due to whelp August	Date bred July	Date due to whelp September	Date bred August	Date due to whelp October	Date bred September	Date due to whelp November	Date bred October	Date due to whelp December	Date bred November	Date due to whelp January	Date bred December	Date due to whelp February
1	5	1	5	1	3	1	3	1	3	1	3	1	2	1	3	1	3	1	3	1	3	1	
2	6	2	6	2	4	2	4	2	4	2	4	2	3	2	4	2	4	2	4	2	4	2	3
3	7	3	7	3	5	3	5	3	5	3	5	3	4	3	5	3	5	3	5	3	5	3	4
4	8	4	8	4	6	4	6	4	6	4	6	4	5	4	6	4	6	4	6	4	6	4	
5	9	5	9	5	7	5	7	5	7	5	7	5	6	5	7	5	7	5	7	5	7	5	
6	10	6	10	6	8	6	8	6	8	6	8	6	7	6	8	6	8	6	8	6	8	6	7
7	11	7	11	7	9	7	9	7	9	7	9	7	8	7	9	7	9	7	9	7	9	7	
8	12	8	12	8	10	8	10	8	10	8	10	8	9	8	10	8	10	8	10	8	10	8	
9	13	9	13	9	11	9	11	9	11	9	11	9	10	9	11	9	11	9	11	9	11	9	10
10	14	10	14	10	12	10	12	10	12	10	12	10	11	10	12	10	12	10	12	10	12	10	11
11	15	11	15	11	13	11	13	11	13	11	13	11	12	11	13	11	13	11	13	11	13	11	12
12	16	12	16	12	14	12	14	12	14	12	14	12	13	12	14	12	14	12	14	12	14	12	13
13	17	13	17	13	15	13	15	13	15	13	15	13	14	13	15	13	15	13	15	13	15	13	14
14	18	14	18	14	16	14	16	14	16	14	16	14	15	14	16	14	16	14	16	14	16	14	15
15	19	15	19	15	17	15	17	15	17	15	17	15	16	15	17	15	17	15	17	15	17	15	16
16	20	16	20	16	18	16	18	16	18	16	18	16	17	16	18	16	18	16	18	16	18	16	17
17	21	17	21	17	19	17	19	17	19	17	19	17	18	17	19	17	19	17	19	17	19	17	18
18	22	18	22	18	20	18	20	18	20	18	20	18	19	18	20	18	20	18	20	18	20	18	
19	23	19	23	19	21	19	21	19	21	19	21	19	20	19	21	19	21	19	21	19	21	19	20
20	24	20	24	20	22	20	22	20	22	20	22	20	21	20	22	20	22	20	22	20	22	20	21
21	25	21	25	21	23	21	23	21	23	21	23	21	22	21	23	21	23	21	23	21	23	21	22
22	26	22	26	22	24	22	24	22	24	22	24	22	23	22	24	22	24	22	24	22	24	22	23
23	27	23	27	23	25	23	25	23	25	23	25	23	24	23	25	23	25	23	25	23	25	23	24
24	28	24	28	24	26	24	26	24	26	24	26	24	25	24	26	24	26	24	26	24	26	24	25
25	29	25	29	25	27	25	27	25	27	25	27	25	26	25	27	25	27	25	27	25	27	25	26
26	30	26	30	26	28	26	28	26	28	26	28	26	27	26	28	26	28	26	28	26	28	26	27
27	31	27	1 (May)	27	29	27	29	27	29	27	29	27	28	27	29	27	29	27	29	27	29	27	
28	1 (Apr.)	28	2	28	30	28	30 (July)	28	30	28	30	28	29	28	30	28	30 (Dec.)	28	30	28	30	28	(Mo...)
29	2			29	31 (June)	29	1	29	31 (Aug.)	29	31 (Sep.)	29	30 (Oct.)	29	31 (Nov.)	29	1	29	31 (Jan.)	29	31 (Feb.)	29	
30	3			30	1	30	2	30	1	30	1	30	1	30	1	30	2	30	1	30	1	30	
31	4			31	2			31	2			31	2	31	2			31	2			31	

THE PREGNANCY AND WHELPING
OF THE BITCH

The "period of gestation" of the bitch, by which is meant the duration of her pregnancy, is usually estimated at sixty-three days. Many bitches, especially young ones, have their puppies as early as sixty days after they are bred. Cases have occurred in which strong puppies were born after only fifty-seven days, and there have been cases that required as many as sixty-six days. However, if puppies do not arrive by the sixty-fourth day, it is time to consult a veterinarian.

For the first five to six weeks of her pregnancy, the bitch requires no more than normal good care and unrestricted exercise. For that period, she needs no additional quantity of food, although her diet must contain sufficient amounts of all the food factors, as is stated in the division of this book that pertains to food. After the fifth to sixth week, the ration must be increased and the violence of exercise restricted. Normal running and walking are likely to be better for the pregnant bitch than a sedentary existence but she should not be permitted to jump, hunt, or fight during the latter half of her gestation. Violent activity may cause her to abort her puppies.

About a week before she is due to whelp, a bed should be prepared for her and she be persuaded to use it for sleeping. This bed may be a box of generous size, big enough to accommodate her with room for activity. It should be high enough to permit her to stand upright, and is better for having a hinged cover. An opening in one side will afford her ingress and egress. This box should be placed in a secluded location, away from any possible molestation by other dogs, animals, or children. The bitch must be made confident of her security in her box.

A few hours, or perhaps a day or two, before her whelping, the bitch will probably begin arranging the bedding of the box to suit herself, tearing blankets or cushions and nosing the parts into the corners. Before the whelping actually starts, however, it is best to substitute burlap sacking, securely tacked to the floor of the box. This is to provide traction for the puppies to reach the dam's breast.

The whelping may take place at night without any assistance from the owner. The box may be opened in the morning to reveal the happy bitch nursing a litter of complacent puppies. But she may need some assistance in her parturition. If whelping is recognized to be in process, it is best to help the bitch.

As the puppies arrive, one by one, the enveloping membranes should be removed as quickly as possible, lest the puppies suffocate. Having removed the membrane, the umbilical cord should be severed with clean scissors some three or four inches from the puppy's belly. (The part of the cord attached to the belly will dry up and drop off in a few days.) There is no need for any medicament or dressing of the cord after it is cut.

The bitch should be permitted to eat the afterbirth if she so desires, and she normally does. If she has no assistance, she will probably remove the membrane and sever the cord with her teeth. The only dangers are that she may delay too long or may bite the cord too short. Some bitches, few of them, eat their newborn puppies (especially bitches not adequately fed during pregnancy). This unlikelihood should be guarded against.

As they arrive, it is wise to remove all the puppies except one, placing them in a box or basket lined and covered by a woolen cloth, somewhere aside or away from the whelping bed, until all have come and the bitch's activity has ceased. The purpose of this is to prevent her from walking or lying on the whelps, and to keep her from being disturbed by the puppies' whining. A single puppy should be left with the bitch to ease her anxiety.

It is best that the "midwife" be somebody with whom the bitch is on intimate terms and in whom she has confidence. Some bitches exhibit a jealous fear and even viciousness while they are whelping. Such animals are few, and most appear grateful for gentle assistance through their ordeal.

The puppies arrive at intervals of a few minutes to an hour until all are delivered. It is wise to call a veterinarian if the interval is greater than one hour. Though such service is seldom needed, an experienced veterinarian can usually be depended upon to withdraw with obstetrical forceps an abnormally presented puppy. It is possible, but unlikely, that the veterinarian will recommend a Caesarian section. This surgery in the dog is not very grave, but it should be performed only by an expert veterinarian. It is unnecessary to describe the process here, or the subsequent management of the patient, since, if a Caesarian section should be necessary, the veterinarian will provide all the needed instructions.

Some bitches, at or immediately after their whelping period, go into a convulsive paralysis, which is called *eclampsia*. This is unlikely if the bitch throughout her pregnancy has had an adequate measure of calcium in her rations. The remedy for eclampsia is the intravenous or intramuscular administration of parenteral calcium. The bitch suspected of having eclampsia should be attended by a veterinarian.

Assuming that the whelping has been normal and without untoward incident, all of the puppies are returned to the bitch, and put, one by one, to the breast, which strong puppies will accept with alacrity. The less handling of puppies for the first four or five hours of their lives, the better. However, the litter should be looked over carefully for possible defectives and discards, which should be destroyed as soon as possible. There is no virtue in rearing hare-lipped, crippled, or mismarked puppies.

It is usually unwise to destroy sound, healthy puppies just to reduce the number in the litter, since it is impossible to sort young puppies for excellence and one may be destroying the best member of the litter, a future champion. Unless a litter is extraordinarily numerous, the dam, if well fed, can probably suckle them all. If it is found that her milk is insufficient, the litter may be artificially fed or may be divided, and the surplus placed on a foster mother if it is possible to obtain one. The foster mother need not be of the same breed as the puppies, a mongrel being as good as any. She should be approximately the same size as the actual mother of the puppies, clean, healthy, and her other puppies should be of as nearly the same age as the ones she is to take over as possible. She should be removed from her own puppies (which may well be destroyed) and her breasts be permitted to fill with milk until she is somewhat uncomfortable, at which time her foster puppies can be put to her breasts and will usually be accepted without difficulty. Unless the services of the foster mother are really required, it is better not to use her.

The whelping bitch may be grateful for a warm meal even between the arrivals of her puppies. As soon as her chore is over, she should be offered food in her box. This should be of cereal and milk or of meat and broth, something sloppy. She will probably not leave her puppies to eat and her meals must be brought to her.

It is wise to give a mild laxative for her bowels, also milk of magnesia. She will be reluctant to get out of her box even to relieve herself for about two days, but she should be urged, even forced, to do so regularly. A sensible bitch will soon settle down to care for her brood and will seldom give further trouble. She should be fed often and well, all that she can be induced to eat during her entire lactation.

As a preventive for infections sometimes occurring after whelping, some experienced breeders and veterinarians recommend injecting the bitch with penicillin or another antibiotic immediately following the birth of the last puppy. Oral doses of the same drug may be given daily thereafter for the first week. It is best to consult your veterinarian about this treatment.

ACID MILK

Occasionally a bitch produces early milk (colostrum) so acid that it disagrees with, sometimes kills, her puppies. The symptoms of the puppies are whining, disquiet, frequently refusal to nurse, frailty, and death. It is true that all milk is slightly acid, and it should be, turning blue litmus paper immersed in it a very light pink. However, milk harmfully on the acid side will readily turn litmus paper a vivid red. It seems that only the first two or three days milk is so affected. Milk problems come also from mastitis and other infections in the bitch.

This is not likely to occur with a bitch that throughout her pregnancy has received an adequate supply of calcium phosphate regularly in her daily ration. That is the best way to deal with the situation—to see to the bitch's correct nutrition in advance of her whelping. The owner has only himself to blame for the bitch's too acid milk, since adequate calcium in advance would have neutralized the acid.

If it is found too late that her milk is too acid, the puppies must be taken from her breast and either given to a foster mother or artificially fed from bottle or by medicine dropper. Artificial feeding of very young puppies seldom is successful. Sometimes the acidity of the dam's milk can be neutralized by giving her large doses of bicarbonate of soda (baking soda), but the puppies should not be restored to her breasts until her milk ceases to turn litmus paper red.

If it is necessary to feed the puppies artificially, "Esbilac," a commercial product, or the following orphan puppy formula, may be used.

7 oz. whole milk
1 oz. cream (top milk)
1 egg yolk
2 tbsp. corn syrup
2 tbsp. lime water

REARING THE PUPPIES

Puppies are born blind and open their eyes at approximately the ninth day thereafter. If they were whelped earlier than the full sixty-three days after the breeding from which they resulted, the difference should be added to the nine days of anticipated blindness. The early eye color of young puppies is no criterion of the color to which the eyes are likely to change, and the breeder's anxiety about his puppies' having light eyes is premature.

In breeds that require the docking of the tail, this should be done on the third day and is a surgical job for the veterinarian. Many a dog has had his tail cut off by an inexperienced person, ruining his good looks and his possibility for a win in the show ring. Dew claws should be removed at the same time. There is little else to do with normal puppies except to let them alone and permit them to grow. The most important thing about their management is their nutrition, which is discussed in another chapter. The first two or three weeks, they will thrive and grow rapidly on their mother's milk, after which they should have additional food as described.

Puppies sleep much of the time, as do other babies, and they should not be frequently awakened to be played with. They grow more and more playful as they mature.

After the second week their nails begin to grow long and sharp. The mother will be grateful if the puppies' nails are blunted with scissors from time to time so that in their pawing of the breast they do not lacerate it. Sharp nails tend to prompt the mother to wean the whelps early, and she should be encouraged to keep them with her as long as she will tolerate them. Even the small amount of milk they can drain from her after the weaning process is begun is the best food they can obtain. It supplements and makes digestible the remainder of their ration.

Many bitches, after their puppies are about four weeks of age, eat and regurgitate food, which is eaten by the puppies. This food is warmed and partly digested in the bitch's stomach. This practice, while it may appear digusting to the novice keeper of dogs, is perfectly normal and should not be discouraged. However, it renders it all the more necessary that the food of the bitch be sound, clean, and nutritious.

It is all but impossible to rear a litter of puppies without their becoming infested with roundworms. Of course, the bitch should be wormed, if she harbors such parasites, before she is bred, and her teats should be thoroughly washed with mild soap just before she whelps to free them from the eggs of roundworms. Every precaution must be taken to reduce the infestation of the puppies to a minimum. But, in spite of all it is possible to do, puppies will have roundworms. These pests hamper growth, reduce the puppies' normal resistance to disease, and may kill them outright unless the worms are eliminated. The worming of puppies is discussed in the chapter entitled "Intestinal Parasites and Their Control."

External Vermin
and Parasites

Under this heading the most common external parasites will be given consideration. Fleas, lice, ticks, and flies are those most commonly encountered and causing the most concern. The external parasite does not pose the problem that it used to before we had the new "miracle" insecticides. Today, with DDT, lindane, and chlordane, the course of extermination and prevention is much easier to follow. Many of the insecticide sprays have a four to six weeks residual effect. Thus the premises can be sprayed and the insect pests can be quite readily controlled.

FLEAS

Neglected dogs are too often beset by hundreds of blood-thirsty fleas, which do not always confine their attacks to the dogs but also sometimes feast upon their masters. Unchecked, they overrun kennels, homes, and playgrounds. Moreover, they are the intermediate hosts for the development of the kind of tapeworm most frequently found in dogs, as will be more fully discussed under the subject of *Intestinal Parasites*. Fleas are all-round bad actors and nuisances. Although it need hardly concern us in America, where the disease is not known to exist, fleas are the recognized and only vectors of bubonic plague.

There are numerous kinds and varieties of fleas, of which we shall discuss here only the three species often found on dogs. These are the human flea (*Pulex irritans*), the dog flea (*Ctenocephalides canis*), and the so-called chicken flea or sticktight flea (*Echidnophaga gallinacea*).

Of these the human flea prefers the blood of man to that of the dog, and unless humans are also bothered, are not likely to be found on the dog. They are small, nearly black insects, and occur mostly in the Mississippi Valley and in California. Their control is the same as for the dog flea.

The dog flea is much larger than his human counterpart, is dark brown in color and seldom bites mankind. On an infested dog these dog fleas may be found buried in the coat of any part of the anatomy, but their choicest habitat is the area of the back just forward from the tail and over the loins. On that part of a badly neglected dog, especially in summer, fleas by the hundreds will be found intermixed with their dung and with dried blood. They may cause the dog some discomfort or none. It must not be credited that because a dog is not kept in a constant or frequent agitation of scratching that he harbors no fleas. The coats of pet animals are soiled and roughened by the fleas and torn by the scratching that they sometimes induce. Fleas also appear to be connected with summer eczema of dogs; at least the diseased condition of the skin often clears up after fleas are eradicated.

Although the adults seldom remain long away from the dog's body, fleas do not reproduce themselves on the dog. Rather, their breeding haunts are the debris, dust, and sand of the kennel floor, and especially the accumulations of dropped hair, sand, and loose soil of unclean sleeping boxes. Nooks and cracks and crannies of the kennel may harbor the eggs or maggot-like larvae of immature fleas.

This debris and accumulation must be eliminated—preferably by incineration—after which all possible breeding areas should be thoroughly sprayed with a residual effect spray.

The adult dog may be combed well, then bathed in a detergent solution, rinsed thoroughly in warm water, and allowed to drip fairly dry. A solution of Pine Oil (1 oz. to a quart of water) is then used as a final rinse. This method of ridding the dog of its fleas is ideal in warm weather. The Pine Oil imparts a pleasant odor to the dog's coat and the animal will enjoy being bathed and groomed.

The same procedure may be followed for young puppies except that the Pine Oil solution should be rinsed off. When bathing is not feasible, then a good flea powder—one containing lindane—should be used.

Sticktight fleas are minute, but are to be found, if at all, in patches on the dog's head and especially on the ears. They remain quiescent and do not jump, as the dog fleas and human fleas do. Their tiny heads are buried in the dog's flesh. To force them loose from the area decapitates them and the heads remain in the skin which is prone to fester from the irritation. They may be dislodged by placing a cotton pad or thick cloth well soaked in ether or alcohol over the flea patch, which causes them immediately to relinquish their hold, after which they can be easily combed loose and destroyed.

These sticktights abound in neglected, dirty, and abandoned chicken houses, which, if the dogs have access to them, should be cleaned out thoroughly and sprayed with DDT.

Fleas, while a nuisance, are only a minor problem. They should be eliminated not only from the dog but from all the premises he inhabits. Dogs frequently are reinfested with fleas from other dogs with which they play or come in contact. Every dog should be occasionally inspected for the presence of fleas, and, if any are found, immediate means should be taken to eradicate them.

LICE

There are even more kinds of lice than of fleas, although as they pertain to dogs there is no reason to differentiate them. They do not infest dogs, except in the events of gross neglect or of unforeseen accident. Lice reproduce themselves on the body of the dog. To rid him of the adult lice is easy. The standard Pine Oil solution used to kill fleas will also kill lice. However, the eggs or "nits" are harder to remove. Weather permitting, it is sometimes best to have the dog clipped of all its hair. In heavily infested dogs this is the only sure way to cope with the situation. When the hair is clipped, most of the "nits" are removed automatically. A good commercial flea and louse powder applied to the skin will then keep the situation under control.

Rare as the occurrence of lice upon dogs may be, they must be promptly treated and eradicated. Having a dog with lice can prove to be embarrassing, for people just do not like to be around anything lousy. Furthermore, the louse may serve as the intermediate host of the tapeworm in dogs.

The dog's quarters should be thoroughly sprayed with a residual spray of the same type recommended for use in the control of fleas. The problem of disinfecting kennel and quarters is not as great as it is in the case of fleas, for the louse tends to stay on its host, not leaving the dog as the flea does.

TICKS

The terms "wood ticks" and "dog ticks," as usually employed, refer to at least eight different species, whose appearances and habits are so similar that none but entomologists are likely to know them apart. It is useless to attempt to differentiate between these various species here, except to warn the reader that the Rocky Mountain spotted fever tick (*Dermacentor andersoni*) is a vector of the human disease for which it is named, as well as of rabbit fever (tularemia), and care must be employed in removing it from dogs lest the hands be infected. Some one or more of these numerous species are to be found in well nigh every state in the Union, although there exist wide areas where wood ticks are seldom seen and are not a menace to dogs.

All the ticks must feed on blood in order to reproduce themselves. The eggs are always deposited on the ground or elsewhere after the female, engorged with blood, has dropped from the dog or other animal upon which she has fed. The eggs are laid in masses in protected places on the ground, particularly in thick clumps of grass. Each female lays only one such mass, which contains 2500 to 5000 eggs. The development of the American dog tick embraces four stages: the egg, the larva or seed tick, the nymph, and the adult. The two intermediate stages in the growth of the tick are spent on rodents, and only in the adult stage does it attach itself to the dog. Both sexes affix themselves to dogs and to other animals and feed on their blood; the males do not increase in size, although the female is tremendously enlarged as she gorges. Mating occurs while the female is feeding. After some five to thirteen days, she drops from her host, lays her eggs and dies. At no time do ticks feed on anything except the blood of animals.

The longevity and hardihood of the tick are amazing. The larvae and nymphs may live for a full year without feeding, and the adults survive for more than two years if they fail to encounter a host to which they may attach. In the Northern United States the adults are most active in the spring and summer, few being found after July. But in the warmer Southern states they may be active the year around.

Although most of the tick species require a vegetative cover and wild animal hosts to complete their development, at least one species, the brown tick (*Rhipicephalus sanguinius*), is adapted to life in the dryer environment of kennels, sheds, and houses, with the dog as its only necessary host. This tick is the vector of canine piroplasmosis, although this disease is at this time almot negligible in the United States.

This brown dog tick often infests houses in large numbers, both immature and adult ticks lurking around baseboards, window casings, furniture, the folds of curtains, and elsewhere. Thus, even dogs kept in houses are sometimes infested with hundreds of larvae, nymphs, and adults of this tick. Because of its ability to live in heated buildings, the species has become established in many Northern areas. Unlike the other tick species, the adult of the brown dog tick does not bite human beings. However, also unlike the other ticks, it is necessary not only to rid the dogs of this particular tick but also to eliminate the pests from their habitat, especially the dogs' beds and sleeping boxes. A spray with a 10% solution of DDT suffices for this purpose. Fumigation of premises seldom suffices, since not only are brown dog ticks very resistant to mere fumigation, but the ticks are prone to lurk around entry ways, porches and outbuildings, where they cannot be reached with a fumigant. The spraying with DDT may not penetrate to spots where some ticks are in hiding, and it must be repeated at intervals until all the pests are believed to be completely eradicated.

Dogs should not be permitted to run in brushy areas known to be infested with ticks, and upon their return from exercise in a place believed to harbor ticks, dogs should be carefully inspected for their presence.

If a dog's infestation is light, the ticks may be picked individually from his skin. To make tick release its grip, dab with alcohol or a drop of ammonia. If the infestation is heavy, it is easier and quicker to saturate his coat with a derris solution (one ounce of soap and two ounces of derris powder dissolved in one gallon of water). The derris should be of an excellent grade containing at least 3% of rotenone. The mixture may be used and reused, since it retains its strength for about three weeks if it is kept in a dark place.

If possible, the dip should be permitted to dry on the dog's coat. It should not get into a dog's eyes. The dip will not only kill the ticks that are attached to the dog, but the powder drying in the hair will repel further infestation for two or three days and kill most if not all the boarders. These materials act slowly, requiring sometimes as much as twenty-four hours to complete the kill.

If the weather is cold or the use of the dip should be otherwise inconvenient, derris powder may be applied as a dust, care being taken that it penetrates the hair and reaches the skin. Breathing or swallowing derris may cause a dog to vomit, but he will not be harmed by it. The dust and liquid should be kept from his eyes.

Since the dog is the principal host on which the adult tick feeds and since each female lays several thousand eggs after feeding, treating the dog regularly will not only bring him immediate relief but will limit the reproduction of the ticks. Keeping underbrush, weeds, and grass closely cut tends to remove protection favorable to the ticks. Burning vegetation accomplishes the same results.

Many of the ticks in an infested area may be killed by the thorough application of a spray made as follows: Four tablespoonfuls of nicotine sulphate (40% nicotine) in three gallons of water. More permanent results may be obtained by adding to this solution four ounces of sodium fluorides, but this will injure the vegetation.

Besides the ticks that attach themselves to all parts of the dog, there is another species that infests the ear specifically. This pest, the spinose ear tick, penetrates deep into the convolutions of the ear and often causes irritation and pain, as evidenced by the dog's scratching its ears, shaking its head or holding it on one side. One part derris powder (5% rotenone) mixed with ten parts medicinal mineral oil and dropped into the ear will kill spinose ear ticks. Only a few drops of the material is required, but it is best to massage the base of the ear to make sure the remedy penetrates to the deepest part of the ear to reach all the ticks.

FLIES

Flies can play havoc with dogs in outdoor kennels, stinging them and biting the ears until they are raw. Until recently the only protection against them was the screening of the entire kennel. The breeding places of flies, which are damp filth and stagnant garbage, are in most areas now happily abated, but the chief agent for control of the pest is DDT.

A spray of a 10% solution of DDT over all surfaces of the kennel property may be trusted to destroy all the flies that light on those surfaces for from two weeks to one month. It must, of course, be repeated from time to time when it is seen that the efficacy of the former treatment begins to diminish.

Intestinal Parasites and
Their Control

THE varieties of worms that may inhabit the alimentary tract of the dog are numerous. Much misapprehension exists, even among experienced dog keepers, about the harm these parasites may cause and about the methods of getting rid of them. Some dog keepers live in terror of these worms and continually treat their dogs for them whether they are known to be present or not; others ignore the presence of worms and do nothing about them. Neither policy is justified.

Promiscuous dosing, without the certainty that the dog harbors worms or what kind he may have, is a practice fraught with danger for the well-being of the animal. All drugs for the expulsion or destruction of parasites are poisonous or irritant to a certain degree and should be administered only when it is known that the dog is infested by parasites and what kind. It is hardly necessary to say that when a dog is known to harbor worms he should be cleared of them, but in most instances there is no such urgency as is sometimes manifested.

It may be assumed that puppies at weaning time are more or less infested with intestinal roundworms or ascarids (*Toxocara canis*) and that such puppies need to be treated for worms. It is all but impossible to rear a litter of puppies to weaning age free from those parasites. Once the puppies are purged of them, it is amazing to see the spurt of their growth and the renewal of their thriftiness.

74

Many neglected puppies surmount the handicap of their worms and at least some of them survive. This, however, is no reason that good puppies—puppies that are worth saving—should go unwormed and neglected.

The ways to find out that a dog actually has worms are to see some of the worms themselves in the dog's droppings or to submit a sample of his feces to a veterinarian or to a biological laboratory for microscopic examination. From a report of such an examination, it is possible to know whether or not a dog is a host to intestinal parasites at all and intelligently to undertake the treatment and control of the specific kind he may harbor.

All of the vermifuges, vermicides, and anthelmintic remedies tend to expel other worms besides the kind for which they are specifically intended, but it is better to employ the remedy particularly effective against the individual kind of parasite the dog is known to have, and to refrain from worm treatment unless or until it is known to be needed.

ROUNDWORMS

The ascarids, or large intestinal roundworms, are the largest of the worm parasites occurring in the digestive tract of the dog, varying in length from 1 to 8 inches, the females being larger than the males. The name "spool worms," which is sometimes applied to them, is derived from their tendency to coil in a springlike spiral when they are expelled, either from the bowel or vomited, by their hosts. There are at least two species of them which frequently parasitize dogs: *Toxocara canis* and *Toxascaris leonina,* but they are so much alike except for some minor details in the life histories of their development that it is not practically necessary for the dog keeper to seek to distinguish between them.

Neither specie requires an intermediate host for its development. Numerous eggs are deposited in the intestinal tract of the host animal; these eggs are passed out by the dog in his feces and are swallowed by the same or another animal, and hatching takes place in its small intestine. Their development requires from twelve to sixteen days under favorable circumstances.

It has been shown that puppies before their birth may be infested by roundworms from their mother. This accounts for the occasional finding of mature or nearly mature worms in very young puppies. It cannot occur if the mother is entirely free from worms, as she should be.

These roundworms are particularly injurious to young puppies. The commonest symptoms of roundworm infestation are general unthriftiness, digestive disturbances, and bloat after feeding. The hair grows dead and lusterless, and the breath may have a peculiar sweetish odor. Large numbers of roundworms may obstruct the intestine, and many have been known to penetrate the intestinal wall. In heavy infestations the worms may wander into the bile ducts, stomach, and even into the lungs and upper respiratory passages where they may cause pneumonia, especially in very young animals.

The control of intestinal roundworms depends primarily upon prompt disposal of feces, keeping the animals in clean quarters and on clean ground, and using only clean utensils for feed and water. Dampness of the ground favors the survival of worm eggs and larvae. There is no known chemical treatment feasible for the destruction of eggs in contaminated soil, but prolonged exposure to sunlight and drying has proved effective.

Numerous remedies have been in successful use for roundworms, including turpentine, which has a recognized deleterious effect upon the kidneys; santonin, an old standby; freshly powdered betel nut and its derivative, arecoline, both of which tend to purge and sicken the patient; oil of chenopodium, made from American wormseed; carbon tetrachloride, widely used as a cleaning agent; tetrachlorethylene, closely related chemically to the former, but less toxic; and numerous other medicaments. While all of them are effective as vermifuges or vermicides, if rightly employed, to each of them some valid objection can be interposed.

In addition to the foregoing, there are other vermifuges available for treatment of roundworms. Some may be purchased without a prescription, whereas others may be procured only when prescribed by a veterinarian.

HOOKWORMS

Hookworms are the most destructive of all the parasites of dogs. There are three species of them—*Ancylostoma caninum, A. braziliense,* and *Uncinaria stenocephalia*—all to be found in dogs in some parts of the United States. The first named is the most widespread; the second found only in the warmer parts of the South and Southwest; the last named, in the North and in Canada. All are similar one to another and to the hookworm that infests mankind (*Ancylostoma uncinariasis*). For purposes of their eradication, no distinction need be made between them.

It is possible to keep dogs for many years in a dry and well drained area without an infestation with hookworms, which are contracted only on infested soils. However, unthrifty dogs shipped from infested areas are suspect until it is proved that hookworm is not the cause of their unthriftiness.

Hookworm males seldom are longer than half an inch, the females somewhat larger. The head end is curved upward, and is equipped with cutting implements, which may be called teeth, by which they attach themselves to the lining of the dog's intestine and suck his blood.

The females produce numerous eggs which pass out in the dog's feces. In two weeks or a little more these eggs hatch, the worms pass through various larval stages, and reach their infective stage. Infection of the dog may take place through his swallowing the organism, or by its penetration of his skin through some lesion. In the latter case the worms enter the circulation, reach the lungs, are coughed up, swallowed, and reach the intestine where their final development occurs. Eggs appear in the dog's feces from three to six weeks after infestation.

Puppies are sometimes born with hookworms already well developed in their intestines, the infection taking place before their birth. Eggs of the hookworm are sometimes found in the feces of puppies only thirteen days old. Assumption is not to be made that all puppies are born with hookworms or even that they are likely to become infested, but in hookworm areas the possibility of either justifies precautions that neither shall happen.

Hookworm infestation in puppies and young dogs brings about a condition often called kennel anemia. There may be digestive disturbances and blood streaked diarrhea. In severe cases the feces may be almost pure blood. Infested puppies fail to grow, often lose weight, and the eyes are sunken and dull. The loss of blood results in an anemia with pale mucous membranes of the mouth and eyes. This anemia is caused by the consumption of the dog's blood by the worms and the bleeding that follows the bites. The worms are not believed to secrete a poison or to cause damage to the dog except loss of blood.

There is an admitted risk in worming young puppies before weaning time, but it is risk that must be run if the puppies are known to harbor hookworms. The worms, if permitted to persist, will ruin the puppies and likely kill them. No such immediacy is needful for the treatment of older puppies and adult dogs, although hookworm infestation will grow steadily worse until it is curbed. It should not be delayed and neglected in the belief or hope that the dog can cure himself.

If treatment is attempted at home, there are available three fairly efficacious and safe drugs that may be used: normal butyl chloride, hexaresorcinal, and methyl benzine.

If a dog is visibly sick and a diagnosis of hookworm infestation has been made, treatment had best be under professional guidance.

Brine made by stirring common salt (sodium chloride) into boiling water, a pound and a half of salt to the gallon of water, will destroy hookworm infestation in the soil. A gallon of brine should be sufficient to treat eight square feet of soil surface. One treatment of the soil is sufficient unless it is reinfested.

TAPEWORMS

The numerous species of tapeworm which infest the dog may, for practical purposes, be divided into two general groups, the armed forms and the unarmed forms. Species of both groups resemble each other in their possession of a head and neck and a chain of segments. They are, however, different in their life histories, and the best manner to deal with each type varies. This is unfortunately not well understood, since to most persons a tapeworm is a tapeworm.

The armed varieties are again divided into the single pored forms of the genera *Taenia, Multiceps,* and *Echinococcus,* and the double pored tapeworm, of which the most widespread and prevalent among dogs in the United States is the so-called dog tapeworm, *Dipylidium caninum.* This is the variety with segments shaped like cucumber-seeds. The adult rarely exceeds a foot in length, and the head is armed with four or five tiny hooks. For the person with well cared for and protected dogs, this is the only tapeworm of which it is necessary to take particular cognizance.

The dog tapeworm requires but a single intermediate host for its development, which in most cases is the dog flea or the biting louse. Thus, by keeping dogs free from fleas and lice the major danger of tapeworm infestation is obviated.

The tapeworm is bi-sexual and requires the intermediate host in order to complete its life cycle. Segments containing the eggs of the tapeworm pass out with the stool, or the detached proglottid may emerge by its own motile power and attach itself to the contiguous hair. The flea then lays its eggs on this segment, thus affording sustenance for the larva. The head of the tapeworm develops in the lung chamber of the baby flea. Thus, such a flea, when it develops and finds its way back to a dog, is the potential carrier of tapeworm. Of course, the cycle is complete when the flea bites the dog and the dog, in biting the area to relieve the itching sensation, swallows the flea.

Since the egg of the tapeworm is secreted in the segment that breaks off and passes with the stool, microscopic examination of the feces is of no avail in attempting to determine whether tapeworms infest a dog. It is well to be suspicious of a finicky eater— a dog that refuses all but the choicest meat and shows very little appetite. The injury produced by this armed tapeworm to the dog that harbors it is not well understood. Frequently it produces no symptoms at all, and it is likely that it is not the actual cause of many of the symptoms attributed to it. At least, it is known that a dog may have one or many of these worms over a long period of time and apparently be no worse for their presence. Nervous symptoms or skin eruptions, or both, are often charged to the presence of tapeworm, which may or may not be the cause of the morbid condition.

Tapeworm-infested dogs sometimes involuntarily pass segments of worms and so soil floors, rugs, furniture, or bedding. The passage by dogs of a segment or a chain of segments via the anus is a frequent cause of the dog's itching, which he seeks to allay by sitting and dragging himself on the floor by his haunches. The segments or chains are sometimes mistakenly called pinworms, but pinworms are a kind of roundworm to which dogs are not subject.

Despite that they may do no harm, few dogs owners care to tolerate tapeworms in their dogs. These worms, it has been definitely established, are not transmissible from dog to dog or to man. Without the flea or the louse, it is impossible for the adult dog tapeworm to reproduce itself, and by keeping dogs free from fleas and lice it is possible to keep them also free from dog tapeworm.

The various unarmed species of tapeworm find their intermediate hosts in the flesh and other parts of various animals, fish, crustacians and crayfish. Dogs not permitted to eat raw meats which have not been officially inspected, never have these worms, and it is needless here to discuss them at length. Hares and rabbits are the intermediate hosts to some of these worms and dogs should not be encouraged to feed upon those animals.

Little is known of the effects upon dogs of infestations of the unarmed tapeworms, but they are believed to be similar to the effects (if any) of the armed species.

The prevention of tapeworm infestation may be epitomized by saying: Do not permit dogs to swallow fleas or lice nor to feed upon uninspected raw meats. It is difficult to protect dogs from such contacts if they are permitted to run at large, but it is to be presumed that persons interested enough in caring for dogs to read this book will keep their dogs at home and protect them.

The several species of tapeworm occurring in dogs are not all removable by the same treatment. The most effective treatment for the removal of the armed species, which is the one most frequently found in the dogs, is arecoline hydrobromide. This drug is a drastic purgative and acts from fifteen to forty-five minutes after its administration. The treatment should be given in the morning after the dog has fasted overnight, and food should be withheld for some three hours after dosing.

Arecoline is not so effective against the double-pored tapeworm as against the other armed species, and it may be necessary to repeat the dose after a few days waiting, since some of the tapeworm heads may not be removed by the first treatment and regeneration of the tapeworm may occur in a few weeks. The estimatedly correct dosage is not stated here, since the drug is so toxic that the dosage should be estimated for the individual dog by a competent veterinarian, and it is better that he should be permitted to administer the remedy and control the treatment.

WHIPWORMS

The dog whipworm (*Trichuris vulpis*) is so called from its fancied resemblance to a tiny blacksnake whip, the front part being slender and hairlike and the hinder part relatively thick. It rarely exceeds three inches in its total length. Whipworms in dogs exist more or less generally throughout the world, but few dogs in the United States are known to harbor them. They are for the most part confined to the caecum, from which they are hard to dislodge, but sometimes spill over into the colon, whence they are easy to dislodge.

The complete life history of the whipworm is not well established, but it is known that no intermediate host is required for its development. The eggs appear to develop in much the same way as the eggs of the large roundworm, but slower, requiring from two weeks to several months for the organisms to reach maturity.

It has not as yet been definitely established that whipworms are the true causes of all the ills of which they are accused. In many instances they appear to cause little damage, even in heavy infestations. A great variety of symptoms of an indefinite sort have been ascribed to whipworms, including digestive disturbances, diarrhea, loss of weight, nervousness, convulsions, and general unthriftiness, but it remains to be proved that whipworms were responsible.

To be effective in its removal of whipworms, a drug must enter the caecum and come into direct contact with them; but the entry of the drug into this organ is somewhat fortuitous, and to increase the chances of its happening, large doses of a drug essentially harmless to the dog must be used. Normal butyl chloride meets this requirement, but it must be given in large doses. Even then, complete clearance of whipworms from the caecum may not be expected; the best to be hoped is that their numbers will be reduced and the morbid symptoms will subside.

Before treatment the dog should be fasted for some eighteen hours, although he may be fed two hours after being treated. It is wise to follow the normal butyl chloride in one hour with a purgative dose of castor oil. This treatment, since it is not expected to be wholly effective, may be repeated at monthly intervals.

The only known means of the complete clearance of whipworms from the dog is the surgical removal of the caecum, which of course should be undertaken only by a veterinary surgeon.

HEART WORMS

Heart worms (*Dirofilaria immitis*) in dogs are rare. They occur largely in the South and Southeast, but their incidence appears to be increasing and cases have been reported along the Atlantic Seaboard as far north as New York. The various species of mosquitoes are known to be vectors of heart worms, although the flea is also accused of spreading them.

The symptoms of heart worm infestation are somewhat vague, and include coughing, shortness of breath and collapse. In advanced cases, dropsy may develop. Nervous symptoms, fixity of vision, fear of light, and convulsions may develop. However, all such symptoms may occur from other causes and it must not be assumed because a dog manifests some of these conditions that he has heart worms. The only way to be sure is a microscopic examination of the blood and the presence or absence of the larvae. Even in some cases where larvae have been found in the blood, post mortem examinations have failed to reveal heart worms in the heart.

Both the diagnosis and treatment of heart worm are functions of the veterinarian. They are beyond the province of the amateur. The drug used is a derivative from antimony known as fuadin, and many dogs are peculiarly susceptible to antimony poisoning. If proper treatment is used by a trained veterinarian, a large preponderance of cases make a complete recovery. But even the most expert of veterinarians may be expected to fail in the successful treatment of a percentage of heart worm infestations. The death of some of the victims is to be anticipated.

LESS FREQUENTLY FOUND WORMS

Besides the intestinal worms that have been enumerated, there exist in some dogs numerous other varieties and species of worms which are of so infrequent occurrence that they require no discussion in a book for the general dog keeper. These include, esophageal worms, lungworms, kidney worms, and eye worms. They are in North America, indeed, so rare as to be negligible.

COCCIDIA

Coccidia are protozoic, microscopic organisms. The forms to which the dog is a host are *Isospora rivolta, I. bigeminia* and *I. felis.* Coccidia eggs, called *oocysts,* can be carried by flies and are picked up by dogs as they lick themselves or eat their stools.

These parasides attack the intestinal wall and cause diarrhea. They are particularly harmful to younger puppies that have been weaned, bringing on fever, running eyes, poor appetite and debilitation as well as the loose stools.

The best prevention is scrupulous cleanliness of the puppy or dog, its surroundings and its playmates whether canine or human. Flies should be eliminated as described in the preceding chapter and stools removed promptly where the dog cannot touch it.

Infection can be confirmed by microscopic examination of the stool. Treatment consists of providing nourishing food, which should be force-fed if necessary, and whatever drug the veterinarian recommends. Puppies usually recover, though occasionally their teeth may be pitted as in distemper.

A dog infected once by one form develops immunity to that form but may be infected by another form.

Skin Troubles

THERE is a tendency on the part of the amateur dog keeper to consider any lesion of the dog's skin to be mange. Mange is an unusual condition in clean, well fed, and well cared for dogs. Eczema occurs much more frequently and is often more difficult to control.

MANGE OR SCABIES

There are at least two kinds of mange that effect dogs—sarcoptic mange and demodectic or red mange, the latter rare indeed and difficult to cure.

Sarcoptic mange is caused by a tiny spider-like mite (*Sarcoptes scabiei canis*) which is similar to the mite that causes human scabies or "itch." Indeed, the mange is almost identical with scabies and is transmissible from dog to man. The mite is approximately 1/100th of an inch in length and without magnification is just visible to acute human sight.

Only the female mites are the cause of the skin irritation. They burrow into the upper layers of the skin, where each lays twenty to forty eggs, which in three to seven days hatch into larvae. These larvae in turn develop into nymphs which later grow into adults. The entire life cycle requires from fourteen to twenty-one days for completion. The larvae, nymphs, and males do not burrow into the skin, but live under crusts and scabs on the surface.

The disease may make its first appearance on any part of the dog's body, although it is usually first seen on the head and muzzle, around the eyes, or at the base of the ears. Sometimes it is first noticed in the armpits, the inner parts of the thighs, the lower abdomen or on the front of the chest. If not promptly treated it may cover the whole body and an extremely bad infestation may cause the death of the dog after a few months.

Red points which soon develop into small blisters are the first signs of the disease. These are most easily seen on the unpigmented parts of the skin, such as the abdomen. As the female mites burrow into the skin, there is an exudation of serum which dries and scabs. The affected parts soon are covered with bran-like scales followed with grayish crusts. The itching is intense, especially in hot weather or after exercise. The rubbing and scratching favor secondary bacterial infections and the formation of sores. The hair may grow matted and fall out, leaving bare spots. The exuded serum decomposes and gives rise to a peculiar mousy odor which increases as the disease develops and which is especially characteristic.

Sarcoptic mange is often confused with demodectic (red) mange, ringworm, or with simple eczema. If there is any doubt about the diagnosis, a microscopic examination of the scrapings of the lesions will reveal the true facts.

It is easy to control sarcoptic mange if it is recognized in its earlier stages and treatment is begun immediately. Neglected, it may be very difficult to eradicate. If it is considered how rapidly the causative mites reproduce themselves, the necessity for early treatment becomes apparent. That treatment consists not only of medication of the dog but also of sterilization of his bedding, all tools and implements used on him, and the whole premises upon which he has been confined. Sarcoptic mange is easily and quickly transmissible from dog to dog, from area to area on the same dog, and even from dog to human.

In some manner which is not entirely understood, an inadequate or unbalanced diet appears to predispose a dog to sarcoptic mange, and few dogs adequately fed and cared for ever contract it. Once a dog has contracted mange, however, improvement in the amount of quality of his food seems not to hasten his recovery.

There are various medications recommended for sarcoptic mange, sulphur ointment being the old standby. However, it is messy, difficult to use, and not always effective. For the treatment of sarcoptic mange, there are available today such insecticides as lindane, chlordane, and DDT. The use of these chemicals greatly facilitates treatment and cure of the dogs affected with mange and those exposed to it.

A bath made by dissolving four ounces of derris powder (containing at least 5% rotenone) and one ounce of soap in one gallon of water has proved effective, especially if large areas of the surface of the dog's skin are involved. All crusts and scabs should be removed before its application. The solution must be well scrubbed into the skin with a moderately stiff brush and the whole animal thoroughly soaked. Only the surplus liquid should be taken off with a towel and the remainder must be permitted to dry on the dog. This bath should be repeated at intervals of five days until all signs of mange have disappeared. Three such baths will usually suffice.

The advantage of such all over treatment is that it protects uninfected areas from infection. It is also a precautionary measure to bathe in this solution uninfected dogs which have been in contact with the infected one.

Isolated mange spots may be treated with oil of lavender. Roll a woolen cloth into a swab with which the oil of lavender can be applied and rubbed in thoroughly for about five minutes. This destroys all mites with which the oil of lavender comes into contact.

Even after a cure is believed to be accomplished, vigilance must be maintained to prevent fresh infestations and to treat new spots immediately if they appear.

DEMODECTIC OR RED MANGE

Demodectic mange, caused by the wormlike mite *Demodex canis,* which lives in the hair follicles and the sebaceous glands of the skin, is difficult to cure. It is a baffling malady of which the prognosis is not favorable. The life cycle of the causative organism is not well understood, the time required from the egg to maturity being so far unknown. The female lays eggs which hatch into young of appearance similar to that of the adult, except that they are smaller and have but three pairs of legs instead of four.

One peculiar feature about demodectic mange is that some dogs appear to be genetically predisposed to it while others do not contract it whatever their contact with infected animals may be. Young animals seem to be especially prone to it, particularly those with short hair. The first evidence of its presence is the falling out of the hair on certain areas of the dog. The spots may be somewhat reddened, and they commonly occur near the eyes, on the hocks, elbows, or toes, although they may be on any part of the dog's body. No itching occurs at the malady's inception, and it never grows so intense as in sarcoptic mange.

In the course of time, the hairless areas enlarge, and the skin attains a copper hue; in severe cases it may appear blue or leadish gray. During this period the mites multiply and small pustules develop. Secondary invasions may occur to complicate the situation. Poisons are formed by the bacteria in the pustules, and the absorption of toxic materials deranges the body functions and eventually affects the whole general health of the dog, leading to emaciation, weakness, and the development of an acrid, unpleasant odor.

This disease is slow and subtle in its development, runs a casual course, and frequently extends over a period of two or even three years. Unless it is treated, it usually terminates in death, although spontaneous recovery occasionally occurs, especially if the dog has been kept on a nourishing diet. As in other skin diseases, correct nutrition plays a major part in recovery from demodectic mange, as it plays an even larger part in its prevention.

It is possible to confuse demodectic mange with sarcoptic mange, fungus infection, acne, or eczema. A definite diagnosis is possible only from microscopic examination of skin scrapings and of material from the pustules. The possibility of demodectic mange, particularly in its earlier stages, is not negated by the failure to find the mites under the microscope, and several examinations may be necessary to arrive at a definite diagnosis.

The prognosis is not entirely favorable. It may appear that the mange is cured and a new and healthy coat may be re-established only to have the disease manifest itself in a new area, and the whole process of treatment must be undertaken afresh.

In the treatment of demodectic mange, the best results have been obtained by the persistent use of benzine hexachloride, chlordane, rotenone, and 2-mercapto benzothiazole. Perseverance is necessary, but even then failure is possible.

EAR MITES OR EAR MANGE

The mites responsible for ear mange (*Ododectes cynotis*) are considerably larger than the ones which cause sarcoptic mange. They inhabit the external auditory canal and are visible to the unaided eye as minute, slowly moving, white objects. Their life history is not known, but is probably similar to that of the mite that causes sarcoptic mange.

These mites do not burrow into the skin, but are found deep in the ear canal, near the eardrum. Considerable irritation results from their presence, and the normal secretions of the ear are interfered with. The ear canal is filled with inflammatory products, modified ear wax, and mites, causing the dog to scratch and rub its ears and to shake its head. While ear mange is not caused by incomplete washing or inefficient drying of the ears, it is encouraged by such negligence.

The ear mange infestation is purely local and is no cause for anxiety. An ointment containing benzine hexachloride is very effective in correcting this condition. The ear should be treated every third or fourth day.

ECZEMA

Eczema is probably the most common of all ailments seen in the dog. Oftentimes it is mistaken for mange or ringworm, although there is no actual relationship between the conditions. Eczema is variously referred to by such names as "hot spots," "fungitch," and "kennel itch."

Some years ago there was near-unanimity of opinion among dog people that the food of the animal was the major contributing factor of eczema. Needless to say, the manufacturers of commercial dog foods were besieged with complaints. Some research on the cause of eczema placed most of the blame on outside environmental factors, and with some help from other sources it was found that a vegetative organism was the causative agent in a great majority of the cases.

Some dogs do show an allergic skin reaction to certain types of protein given to them as food, but this is generally referred to as the "foreign protein" type of dermatitis. It manifests itself by raising numerous welts on the skin, and occasionally the head, face, and ears will become alarmingly swollen. This condition can be controlled by the injection of antihistamine products and subsequent dosage with antihistaminic tablets or capsules such as chlortrimenton or benedryl. Whether "foreign protein" dermatitis is due to an allergy or whether it is due to some toxin manufactured and elaborated by the individual dog is a disputed point.

Most cases of eczema start with reddening of the skin in certain parts. The areas most affected seem to be the region along the spine and at the base of the tail. In house dogs this may have its inception from enlarged and plugged anal glands. The glands when full and not naturally expressed are a source of irritation. The dog will rub his hind parts on the grass in order to alleviate the itching sensation. Fleas, lice, and ticks may be inciting factors, causing the dog to rub and roll in the grass in an attempt to scratch the itchy parts.

In hunting dogs, it is believed that the vegetative cover through which the dogs hunt causes the dermatitis. In this class of dogs the skin becomes irritated and inflamed in the armpits, the inner surfaces of the thighs, and along the belly. Some hunting dogs are bedded down in straw or hay, and such dogs invariably show a general reddening of the skin and a tendency to scratch.

As a general rule, the difference between moist and dry eczema lies in the degree to which the dog scratches the skin with his feet or chews it with his teeth. The inflammation ranges from a simple reddening of the skin to the development of papules, vesicles, and pustules with a discharge. Crusts and scabs like dandruff may form, and if the condition is not treated, it will become chronic and then next to impossible to treat with any success. In such cases the skin becomes thickened and may be pigmented. The hair follicles become infected, and the lesions are constantly inflamed and exuding pus.

When inflammation occurs between the toes and on the pads of the feet, it closely resembles "athletes foot" in the human. Such inflammation generally causes the hair in the region to turn a reddish brown. The ears, when they are affected, emit a peculiar moldy odor and exude a brownish black substance. It is thought that most cases of canker of the ear are due to a primary invasion of the ear canal by a vegetative fungus. If there is a pustular discharge, it is due to the secondary pus-forming bacteria that gain a foothold after the resistance of the parts is lowered by the fungi.

Some breeds of dogs are more susceptible to skin ailments than are others. However, all breeds of dogs are likely to show some degree of dermatitis if they are exposed to causative factors.

Most cases of dermatitis are seen in the summer time, which probably accounts for their being referred to as "summer itch" or "hot spots." The warm moist days of summer seem to promote the growth and development of both fleas and fungi. When the fleas bite the dog, the resulting irritation causes the dog to scratch or bite to alleviate the itch. The area thus becomes moist and makes a perfect place for fungi spores to propagate. That the fungi are the cause of the trouble seems evident, because most cases respond when treated externally with a good fungicide. Moreover, the use of a powder containing both an insecticide and a fungicide tends to prevent skin irritation. Simply dusting the dog once or twice a week with a good powder of the type mentioned is sound procedure in the practice of preventive medicine.

(Editor's note: I have had some success with hydrogen peroxide in treating mild skin troubles. Saturate a cotton pad with a mixture of 2 parts 3% hydrogen peroxide to 1 part boiled water. Apply, but do NOT rub, to affected skin. Let dry naturally and when *completely* dry apply an antiseptic talcum powder like Johnson & Johnson's Medicated Powder. When this treatment was suggested to my veterinarian, he confirmed that he had had success with it. If the skin irritation is not noticeably better after two of these treatments, once daily, the case should be referred to a veterinarian.)

RINGWORM

Ringworm is a communicable disease of the skin of dogs, readily transmissible to man and to other dogs and animals. The disease is caused by specific fungi, which are somewhat similar to ordinary molds. The lesions caused by ringworm usually first appear on the face, head, or legs of the dog, but they may occur on any part of the surface of his body.

The disease in dogs is characterized by small, circular areas of dirty gray or brownish-yellow crusts or scabs partially devoid of hair, the size of a dime. As the disease progresses, the lesions increase both in size and in number and merge to form larger patches covered with crusts containing broken off hair. A raw, bleeding surface may appear when crusts are broken or removed by scratching or rubbing to relieve itching. In some cases, however, little or no itching is manifested. Microscopic examination and culture tests are necessary for accurate diagnosis.

If treatment of affected dogs is started early, the progress of the disease can be immediately arrested. Treatment consists of clipping the hair from around the infected spots, removing the scabs and painting the spots with tincture of iodine, five percent salicylic acid solution, or other fungicide two or three times weekly until recovery takes place. In applying these remedies it is well to cover the periphery of the circular lesion as well as its center, since the spots tend to expand outward from their centers. Scabs, hair, and debris removed from the dog during his treatments should be burned to destroy the causative organisms and to prevent reinfection. Precautions in the handling of animals affected with ringworm should be observed to preclude transmission to man and other animals. Isolation of affected dogs is not necessary if the treatment is thorough.

COAT CARE

Skin troubles can often be checked and materially alleviated by proper grooming. Every dog is entitled to the minimum of weekly attention to coat, skin and ears; ideally, a daily stint with brush and comb is highly recommended. Frequent examination may catch skin disease in its early stages and provide a better chance for a quick cure.

The outer or "guard" hairs of a dog's coat should glint in the sunlight. There should be no mats or dead hair in the coat. Wax in the outer ear should be kept at a minimum.

It is helpful to stand the dog on a flat, rigid surface off the floor at a height convenient to the groomer. Start at the head and ears brushing briskly *with* the lay of short hair, *against* the lay of long hair at first then with it. After brushing, use a fine comb with short teeth on fine, short hair and a coarse comb with long teeth on coarse or long hair. If mats cannot be readily removed with brush or comb, use barber's thinning shears and cut into the matted area several times until mat pulls free easily. Some mats can be removed with the fingers if one has the patience to separate the hair a bit at a time.

After brushing and combing, run your palms over the dog's coat from head to tail. Natural oils in your skin will impart sheen to your dog's coat.

The ears of some dogs secrete and exude great amounts of wax. Frequent examination will determine when your dog's ears need cleaning. A thin coating of clean, clear wax is not harmful. But a heavy accumulation of dirty, dark wax needs removal by cotton pads soaked in diluted hydrogen peroxide (3% cut in half with boiled water), or alcohol or plain boiled water if wax is not too thick.

There are sprays, "dry" bath preparations and other commercial products for maintaining your dog's coat health. Test them first, and if they are successful, you may find them beneficial time-savers in managing your dog's coat.

First Aid

JOHN STEINBECK, the Nobel Prize winning author, in *Travels with Charley in Search of America* bemoans the lack of a good, comprehensive book of home dog medicine. Charley is the aged Poodle that accompanies his illustrious author-owner on a motor tour of the U.S.A.

As in human medicine, most treatment and dosing of dogs are better left in the experienced, trained hands and mind of a professional—in this case, the veterinarian. However, there are times and situations when professional aid is not immediately available and an owner's prompt action may save a life or avoid permanent injury. To this purpose, the following suggestions are given.

The First Aid Kit

For instruments keep on hand a pair of tweezers, a pair of pliers, straight scissors, a rectal thermometer, a teaspoon, a tablespoon, and swabs for cotton.

For dressings, buy a container of cotton balls, a roll of cotton and a roll of 2" gauze. Strips of clean, old sheets may come in handy.

For medicines, stock ammonia, aspirin, brandy, 3% hydrogen peroxide, bicarbonate of soda, milk of bismuth, mineral oil, salt, tea, vaseline, kaopectate, baby oil and baby talcum powder.

Handling the Dog for Treatment

Approach any injured or sick dog calmly with reassuring voice and gentle, steady hands. If the dog is in pain, slip a gauze or sheet strip noose over its muzzle tying the ends first under the throat and then back of the neck. Make sure the dog's lips are not caught between his teeth, but make noose around muzzle *tight*.

If the dog needs to be moved, grasp the loose skin on the back of the neck with one hand and support chest with the other hand. If the dog is too large to move in this manner, slide him on a large towel, blanket or folded sheet which may serve as a stretcher for two to carry.

If a pill or liquid is to be administered, back the dog in a corner in a sitting position. For a pill, pry back of jaws apart with thumb and forefinger of one hand and with the same fingers of your other hand place pill as far back in dog's throat as possible; close and hold jaws, rubbing throat to cause swallowing. If dog does not gulp, hold one hand over nostrils briefly; he will gulp for air and swallow pill. For liquids, lift the back of the upper lip and tip spoon into the natural pocket formed in the rear of the lower lip; it may be necessary to pull this pocket out with forefinger. Do not give liquids by pouring directly down the dog's throat; this might choke him or make the fluid go down the wrong way.

After treatment keep dog quiet, preferably in his bed or a room where he cannot injure himself or objects.

Bites and Wounds

Clip hair from area. Wash gently with pure soap and water or hydrogen peroxide. If profuse bleeding continues, apply sheet strip or gauze tourniquet between wound and heart but nearest the wound. Release tourniquet briefly at ten-minute intervals. Cold water compresses may stop milder bleeding.

For insect bites and stings, try to remove stinger with tweezers or a dab of cotton, and apply a few drops of ammonia. If dog is in pain, give aspirin at one grain per 10 pounds. (An aspirin tablet is usually 5 grains.)

Burns

Clip hair from area. Apply strong, lukewarm tea (for its tannic acid content) on a sheet strip compress. Vaseline may be used for slight burns. Give aspirin as recommended if dog is in pain. Keep him warm if he seems to be in shock.

Constipation

Give mineral oil: one-quarter teaspoon up to 10 pounds; half teaspoon from 10 to 25 pounds; full teaspoon from 25 to 75 pounds; three-quarters tablespoon over 75 pounds.

Diarrhea

Give kaopectate in same doses by size as indicated for mineral oil above, but repeat within four and eight hours.

Fighting

Do not try forcibly to separate dogs. If available throw a pail of cold water on them. A sharp rap on the rump of each combatant with a strap or stick may help. A heavy towel or blanket dropped over the head of the aggressor, or a newspaper twisted into a torch, lighted and held near them, may discourage the fighters. If a lighted newspaper is used, be careful that sparks do not fall or blow on dogs.

Fits

Try to get the dog into a room where he cannot injure himself. If possible, cover him with a towel or blanket. When the fit ends, give aspirin one grain for every 10 pounds.

Nervousness

Remove cause or remove the dog from the site of the cause. Give the recommended dose of aspirin. Aspirin acts as a tranquilizer.

Poisoning

If container of the poison is handy, use recommended antidote printed thereon. Otherwise, make a strong solution of household salt in water and force as much as possible into the dog's throat using the lip pocket method. Minutes count with several poisons; if veterinarian cannot be reached immediately, try to get dog to an MD or registered nurse.

Shock

If dog has chewed electric cord, protect hand with rubber glove or thick dry towel and pull cord from socket. If dog has collapsed, hold ammonia under its nose or apply artificial respiration as follows: place dog on side with its head low, press on abdomen and rib cage, releasing pressure at one- or two-second intervals. Keep dog warm.

Stomach Upsets

For mild stomach disorders, milk of bismuth in same doses as recommended for mineral oil under *Constipation* will be effective. For more severe cases brandy in the same doses but diluted with an equal volume of water may be helpful.

Swallowing Foreign Objects

If object is still in mouth or throat, reach in and remove it. If swallowed, give strong salt solution as for *Poisoning.* Some objects that are small, smooth or soft may not give trouble.

Porcupines and Skunks

Using tweezers or pliers, twist quills one full turn and pull out. Apply hydrogen peroxide to bleeding wounds. For skunk spray, wash dog in tomato juice.

WARNING! Get your dog to a veterinarian *soonest* for severe bites, wounds, burns, poisoning, fits and shock.

Internal Canine Diseases
and Their Management

THE word *management* is employed in this chapter heading rather than *treatment,* since the treatment of disease in the dog is the function of the veterinarian, and the best counsel it is possible to give the solicitous owner of a sick dog is to submit the case to the best veterinarian available and to follow his instructions implicitly. In general, it may be said, the earlier in any disease the veterinarian is consulted, the more rapid is the sick animal's recovery and the lower the outlay of money for the services of the veterinarian and for the medicine he prescribes.

Herein are presented some hints for the prevention of the various canine maladies and for their recognition when they occur. In kennel husbandry, disease is a minor problem, and, if preventive methods are employed, it is one that need not be anticipated.

DISTEMPER

Distemper, the traditional bugbear of keeping dogs, the veritable scourge of dog-kind, has at long last been well conquered. Compared with some years ago when "over distemper" was one of the best recommendations for the purchase of a dog, the incidence of distemper in well-bred and adequately cared for dogs is now minimal.

The difference between then and now is that we now have available preventive sera, vaccines, and viruses, which may be employed to forestall distemper before it ever appears. There are valid differences of opinion about which of these measures is best to use and at what age of the dog they are variously indicated. About the choice of preventive measures and the technique of administering them, the reader is advised to consult his veterinarian and to accept his advice. There can be no doubt, however, that any person with a valued or loved young dog should have him immunized.

For many years most veterinarians used the so-called "three-shot" method of serum, vaccine and virus, spaced two weeks apart after the puppy was three or four months old, for permanent immunization. For temporary immunization lasting up to a year, some veterinarians used only vaccine; this was repeated annually if the owner wished, though since a dog was considered most susceptible to distemper in the first year of his life, the annual injection was often discontinued. Under both these methods, serum was used at two-week intervals from weaning to the age when permanent or annual immunization was given.

Until 1950 living virus, produced by the methods then known to and used by laboratories, was considered too dangerous to inject without the preparation of the dog for it by prior use of serum or vaccine (killed virus). Then, researchers in distemper developed an attenuated or weakened live virus by injecting strong virus into egg embryos and other intermediate hosts. The weakened virus is now often used for permanent, one-shot distemper immunization of puppies as young as eight weeks.

Today certain researchers believe that the temporary immunity given by the bitch to her young depends on her own degree of immunity. If she has none, her puppies have none; if she has maximum immunity, her puppies may be immune up to the age of 12 weeks or more. By testing the degree of the bitch's immunity early in her pregnancy, these researchers believe they can determine the proper age at which her puppies should receive their shots.

The veterinarian is best qualified to determine the method of distemper immunization and the age to give it.

Canine distemper is an acute, highly contagious, febrile disease caused by a filterable virus. It is characterized by a catarrhal inflammation of all the mucous membranes of the body, frequently

100

accompanied by nervous symptoms and pustular eruptions of the skin. Its human counterpart is influenza, which, though not identical with distemper, is very similar to it in many respects. Distemper is so serious and complicated a disease as to require expert attention; when a dog is suspected of having it, a veterinarian should be consulted immediately. It is the purpose of this discussion of the malady rather to describe it that its recognition may be possible than to suggest medication for it or means of treating it.

Distemper is known in all countries and all parts of the United States in all seasons of the year, but it is most prevalent during the winter months and in the cold, damp weather of early spring and late autumn. No breed of dogs is immune. Puppies of low constitutional vigor, pampered, overfed, unexercised dogs, and those kept in overheated, unventilated quarters contract the infection more readily and suffer more from it than hardy animals, properly fed and living in a more natural environment. Devitalizing influences which decrease the resistance of the dog, such as rickets, parasitic infestations, unsanitary quarters, and especially an insufficient or unbalanced diet, are factors predisposing to distemper.

While puppies as young as ten days or two weeks have been known to have true cases of distemper, and very old dogs in rare instances, the usual subjects of distemper are between two months (after weaning) and full maturity at about eighteen months. The teething period of four to six months is highly critical. It is believed that some degree of temporary protection from distemper is passed on to a nursing litter through the milk of the mother.

As was first demonstrated by Carré in 1905 and finally established by Laidlaw and Duncan in their work for the Field Distemper Fund in 1926 to 1928, the primary causative agent of distemper is a filterable virus. The clinical course of the disease may be divided into two parts, produced respectively by the primary Carré filterable virus and by a secondary invasion of bacterial organisms which produce serious complicating conditions usually associated with the disease. It is seldom true that uncomplicated Carré distemper would cause more than a fever with malaise and indisposition if the secondary bacterial invasion could be avoided. The primary disease but prepares the ground for the secondary invasion which produces the havoc and all too often kills the patient.

Although it is often impossible to ascertain the source of infection

101

in outbreaks of distemper, it is known that the infection may spread from affected to susceptible dogs by either direct or indirect contact. The disease, while highly infectious throughout its course, is especially easy to communicate in its earliest stages, even before clinical symptoms are manifested. The virus is readily destroyed by heat and by most of the common disinfectants in a few hours, but it resists drying and low temperatures for several days, and has been known to survive freezing for months.

The period of incubation (the time between exposure to infection and the development of the first symptoms) is variable. It has been reported to be as short as three days and as long as two weeks. The usual period is approximately one week. The usual course of the disease is about four weeks, but seriously complicated cases may prolong themselves to twelve weeks.

The early symptoms of distemper, as a rule, are so mild and subtle as to escape the notice of any but the most acute observer. These first symptoms may be a rise in temperature, a watery discharge from the eyes and nose, an impaired appetite, a throat-clearing cough, and a general sluggishness. In about a week's time the symptoms become well marked, with a discharge of mucus or pus from the eyes and nose, and complications of a more or less serious nature, such as broncho-pneumonia, hemorrhagic inflammation of the gastro-intestinal tract, and disturbances of the brain and spinal cord, which may cause convulsions. In the early stages of distemper the body temperature may suddenly rise from the normal 101°F. to 103°. Shivering, dryness of the nostrils, a slight dry cough, increased thirst, a drowsy look, reluctance to eat, and a desire to sleep may follow. Later, diarrhea (frequently streaked with blood or wholly of blood), pneumonia, convulsions, paralysis, or chorea (a persistent twitching condition) may develop. An inflammation of the membranes of the eye may ensue; this may impair or destroy the sight through ulceration or opacity of the cornea. Extreme weakness and great loss of body weight occur in advanced stages.

All, any, or none of these symptoms may be noticeable. It is believed that many dogs experience distemper in so mild a form as to escape the owner's observation. Because of its protean and obscure nature and its strong similarity to other catarrhal affections, the diagnosis of distemper, especially in its early stages, is difficult. In young dogs that are known to have been exposed to the disease, a rise of body temperature, together with shivering, sneezing, loss of appetite, eye and nasal discharge, sluggishness, and diarrhea (all or any of these symptoms), are indicative of trouble.

There is little specific that can be done for a dog with primary distemper. The treatment is largely concerned with alleviating the symptoms. No drug or combination of drugs is known at this time that has any specific action on the disease. Distemper runs a definite course, no matter what is done to try to cure it.

Homologous anti-distemper serum, administered subcutaneously or intravenously by the veterinarian, is of value in lessening the severity of the attack. The veterinarian may see fit to treat the secondary pneumonia with penicillin or one of the sulpha drugs, or to allay the secondary intestinal infection with medication. It is best to permit him to manage the case in his own way. The dog is more prone to respond to care in his own home and with his own people, if suitable quarters and adequate nursing are available to him. Otherwise, he is best off in a veterinary hospital.

The dog affected with distemper should be provided with clean, dry, warm but not hot, well ventilated quarters. It should be given moderate quantities of nourishing, easily digested food—milk, soft boiled eggs, cottage cheese, and scraped lean beef. The sick dog should not be disturbed by children or other dogs. Discharges from eyes and nose should be wiped away. The eyes may be bathed with boric acid solution, and irritation of the nose allayed with greasy substances such as petrolatum. The dog should not be permitted to get wet or chilled, and he should have such medication as the veterinarian prescribes and no other.

When signs of improvement are apparent, the dog must not be given an undue amount of food at one meal, although he may be fed at frequent intervals. The convalescing dog should be permitted to exercise only very moderately until complete recovery is assured.

In the control of distemper, affected animals should be promptly isolated from susceptible dogs. After the disease has run its course, whether it end in recovery or death, the premises where the patient has been kept during the illness should be thoroughly cleaned and disinfected, as should all combs, brushes, or other utensils used on the dog, before other susceptible dogs are brought in. After an apparent recovery has been made in the patient, the germs are present for about four weeks and can be transmitted to susceptible dogs.

CHOREA OR ST. VITUS DANCE

A frequent sequela of distemper is chorea, which is characterized by a more or less pronounced and frequent twitching of a muscle or muscles. There is no known remedy for the condition. It does not impair the usefulness of a good dog for breeding, and having a litter of puppies often betters or cures chorea in the bitch. Chorea is considered a form of unsoundness and is penalized in the show ring. The condition generally becomes worse.

ECLAMPSIA OR WHELPING TETANY

Convulsions of bitches before, during, or shortly after their whelping are called eclampsia. It seldom occurs to a bitch receiving a sufficient amount of calcium and vitamin D in her diet during her pregnancy. The symptoms vary in their severity for nervousness and mild convulsions to severe attacks which may terminate in coma and death. The demands of the nursing litter for calcium frequently depletes the supply in the bitch's system.

Eclampsia can be controlled by the hypodermic administration of calcium gluconate. Its recurrence is prevented by the addition to the bitch's ration of readily utilized calcium and vitamin D.

RICKETS, OR RACHITIS

The failure of the bones of puppies to calcify normally is termed rickets, or more technically rachitis. Perhaps more otherwise excellent puppies are killed or ruined by rickets than by any other disease. It is essentially a disease of puppies, but the malformation of the skeleton produced by rickets persists through the life of the dog.

The symptoms of rickets include lethargy, arched neck, crouched stance, knobby and deformed joints, bowed legs, and flabby muscles. The changes characteristic of defective calcification in the puppy are most marked in the growth of the long bones of the leg, and at the cartilaginous junction of the ribs. In the more advanced stages of rickets the entire bone becomes soft and easily deformed or broken. The development of the teeth is also retarded.

Rickets results from a deficiency in the diet of calcium, phosphorus, or vitamin D. It may be prevented by the inclusion of sufficient amounts of those substances in the puppy's diet. It may also be cured, if not too far advanced, by the same means, although distortions in the skeleton that have already occurred are seldom rectified. The requirements of vitamin D to be artificially supplied are greater for puppies raised indoors and with limited exposure to sunlight or to sunlight filtered through window glass.

(It is possible to give a dog too much vitamin D, but very unlikely without deliberate intent.)

Adult dogs that have had rickets in puppyhood and whose recovery is complete may be bred from without fear of their transmission to their puppies of the malformations of their skeletons produced by the disease. The same imbalance or absence from their diet that produced rickets in the parent may produce it in the progeny, but the disease in such case is reproduced and not inherited.

The requirements of adult dogs for calcium, phosphorus, and vitamin D are much less than for puppies and young dogs, but a condition called osteomalacia, or late rickets, is sometimes seen in grown dogs as the result of the same kind of nutritional deficiency that causes rickets in puppies. In such cases a softening of the bones leads to lameness and deformity. The remedy is the same as in the rickets of puppyhood, namely the addition of calcium, phosphorus, and vitamin D to the diet. It is especially essential that bitches during pregnancy and lactation have included in their diets ample amounts of these elements, both for their own nutrition and for the adequate skeletal formations of their fetuses and the development of their puppies.

BLACKTONGUE

Blacktongue (the canine analogue of pellagra in the human) is no longer to be feared in dogs fed upon an adequate diet. For many years, it was a recognized scourge among dogs, and its cause and treatment were unknown. It is now known to be caused solely by the insufficiency in the ration of vitamin B complex and specifically by an insufficiency of nicotinic acid. (Nicotinic acid is vitamin B_2, formerly known as vitamin G.)

Blacktongue may require a considerable time for its full development. It usually begins with a degree of lethargy, a lack of appetite for the kind of food the dog has been receiving, constipation, often with spells of vomiting, and particularly with a foul odor from the mouth. As the disease develops, the mucous membranes of the mouth, gums, and tongue grow red and become inflamed, with purple splotches of greater or lesser extent, especially upon the front part of the tongue, and with ulcers and pustules on the lips and the lining of the cheeks. Constipation may give way to diarrhea as the disease develops. Blacktongue is an insidious malady, since its development is so gradual.

This disease is unlikely to occur except among dogs whose owners are so unenlightened, careless, or stingy as to feed their dogs exclusively on a diet of cornmeal mush, salt pork, cowpeas, sweet potatoes, or other foodstuffs that are known to be responsible for the development of pellagra in mankind. Blacktongue is not infectious or contagious, although the same deficiency in the diet of dogs may produce the malady in all the inmates throughout a kennel.

Correct treatment involves no medication as such, but consists wholly in the alteration of the diet to include foods which are good sources of the vitamin B complex, including nicotinic acid; such food as the muscles of beef, mutton, or horse, dried yeast, wheat germ, milk, eggs, and especially fresh liver. As an emergency treatment, the hypodermic injection of nicotinic acid may be indicated. Local treatments of the mouth, its cleansing and disinfection, are usually included, although they will avail nothing without the alteration in the diet.

LEPTOSPIROSIS OR CANINE TYPHUS

Leptospirosis, often referred to as canine typhus, is believed to be identical with Weil's disease (infectious jaundice) in the human species. It is not to be confused with non-infectious jaundice in the dog, which is a mere obstruction in the bile duct which occurs in some liver and gastric disorders. Leptospirosis is a comparatively rare disease as yet, but its incidence is growing and it is becoming more widespread.

It is caused by either of two spirocheates, *Leptospira canicola* or *Leptospira icterohenorrhagiae*. These causative organisms are found in the feces or urine of infected rats, and the disease is transmitted to dogs by their ingestion of food fouled by those rodents. It is therefore wise in rat infested houses to keep all dog food in covered metal containers to which it is impossible for rats to gain access. It is also possible for an ill dog to transmit the infection to a well one, and, it is believed, to man. Such cases, however, are rare.

Symptoms of leptospirosis include a variable temperature, vomiting, loss of appetite, gastroenteritis, diarrhea, jaundice and depression. Analysis of blood and urine may be helpful toward diagnosis. The disease is one for immediate reference to the veterinarian whenever suspected.

Prognosis is not entirely favorable, especially if the disease is neglected in its earlier stages. Taken in its incipience, treatment with penicillin has produced excellent results, as has antileptospiral serum and vaccine.

Control measures include the extermination of rats in areas where the disease is known to exist, and the cleaning and disinfection of premises where infected dogs have been kept.

INFECTIOUS HEPATITIS

This is a virus disease attacking the liver. Apparently it is not the same virus that causes hepatitis in humans. Symptoms include an unusual thirst, loss of appetite, vomiting, diarrhea, pain causing the dog to moan, anemia and fever. The afflicted dog may try to hide.

The disease runs a fast course and is often fatal. A dog recovering from it may carry the virus in his urine for a long period, thus infecting other dogs months later.

Serum and vaccine are available to offer protection. A combination for distemper and hepatitis is now offered.

TURNED-IN OR TURNED-OUT EYELIDS

When the eyelid is inverted, or turned-in, it is technically termed entropion. When the eyelid is turned-out, it is referred to as extropion. Both conditions seem to be found in certain strains of dogs and are classified as being heritable. Both conditions may be corrected by competent surgery. It is possible to operate on such cases and have complete recovery without scar formation. However, cognizance should be taken of either defect in a dog to be used for breeding purposes.

CONJUNCTIVITIS OR INFLAMMATION OF THE EYE

Certain irritants, injuries or infections, and many febrile diseases, such as distemper, produce conjunctivitis, an inflammation of the membranes lining the lids of the dog's eyes. At first there is a slight reddening of the membranes and a watery discharge. As the condition progresses, the conjunctivae become more inflamed looking and the color darkens. The discharge changes consistency and color, becoming muco-purulent in character and yellow in color. The eyelids may be pasted shut and granulation of the lids may follow.

When eye infection persists for an extended period of time, the cornea sometimes becomes involved. Ulcers may develop, eventually penetrating the eyeball. When this happens, the condition becomes very painful and, even worse, often leads to the loss of vision.

Home treatment, to be used only until professional care may be had, consists of regular cleaning of the eye with a 2% boric acid solution and the application of one of the antibiotic eye ointments.

When anything happens to the dog's eye, it is always best to seek professional help and advice.

RABIES

This disease, caused by a virus, is transmissible to all warm blooded animals, and the dog seems to be the number one disseminator of the virus. However, outbreaks of rabies have been traced to wild animals—the wolf, coyote, or fox biting a dog which in turn bites people, other dogs, or other species of animals.

The virus, which is found in the saliva of the rabid animal, enters the body only through broken skin. This usually is brought about by biting and breaking the skin, or through licking an open cut on the skin. The disease manifests itself clinically in two distinct forms. One is called the "furious type" and the other the "dumb type." Both types are produced by the same strain of virus.

The disease works rather peculiarly on the dog's disposition and character. The kindly old dog may suddenly become ferocious; just the reverse may also occur, the mean, vicious dog becoming gentle and biddable. At first the infected dog wants to be near his master, wants to lick his hand or his boots; his appetite undergoes a sudden change, becoming voracious, and the animal will eat anything— stones, bits of wood, even metal. Soon there develops a sense of wanderlust, and the dog seems to wish to get as far away as possible from his owner.

In all rabid animals there is an accentuation of the defense mechanisms. In other words, the dog will bite, the cat will hiss and claw, the horse will bite and kick, and the cow will attack anything that moves.

An animal afflicted with rabies cannot swallow because there is usually a paralysis of the muscles of deglutinition. The animal, famished for a drink, tries to bite the water or whatever fluid he may be attempting to drink. The constant champing of the jaws causes the saliva to become mixed and churned with air, making it appear whipped and foamy. In the old days when a dog "frothed at the mouth," he was considered "mad." There is no doubt but what some uninfected dogs have been suspected of being rabid and shot to death simply because they exhibited these symptoms.

One of the early signs of rabies in the dog is the dropping of the lower jaw. This is a sign of rabies of the so-called "dumb type." The animal has a "faraway" look in his eyes, and his voice or bark has an odd pitch. Manifesting these symptoms, the dog is often taken to the clinic by the owner, who is sure the dog has a bone in the throat. The hind legs, and eventually the whole hindquarters, subsequently become paralyzed, and death ensues.

Many commonwealths have passed laws requiring that all dogs be vaccinated against rabies, and usually, a vaccination certificate must be presented before a dog license may be issued. The general enforcement of this law alone would go a long way toward the eradication of rabies.

Some will ask why a dog must be impounded as a biter when he has taken a little "nip" at someone and merely broken the skin— if this must be done, they cannot understand the "good" of the vaccination. But the vaccination does not give the dog the right to bite. Statistics show that rabies vaccination is effective in about 88% of the cases. All health authorities wish it were 100% effective, thus eliminating a good deal of worry from their minds. Because the vaccination is not 100% effective, we cannot take a chance on the vaccine alone. The animal must be impounded and under the daily supervision of a qualified observer, generally for a period of fourteen days. It is pretty well recognized that if the bite was provocated by rabies, the biting animal will develop clinical symptoms in that length of time; otherwise, he will be released as "clinically normal."

THE SPAYING OF BITCHES

The spaying operation, technically known as an ovariectomy, is the subject of a good deal of controversy. It is an operation that has its good and its bad points.

Spayed bitches cannot be entered in the show ring, and of course can never reproduce their kind. However, under certain circumstances, the operation is recommended by veterinarians. If the operation is to be performed, the bitch should preferably be six to eight months of age. At this age, she has pretty well reached the adolescent period; time enough has been allowed for the endocrine balance to become established and the secondary sex organs to develop.

Mechanical difficulties sometimes arise in the urinary systems of bitches that have been operated on at three or four months of age. In a very small percentage of the cases, loss of control of the sphincter muscles of the bladder is observed. But this can readily be corrected by an injection of the female hormone stilbestrol.

There are many erroneous ideas as to what may happen to the female if she is spayed. Some people argue that the disposition will be changed, that the timid dog may become ferocious, and, strangely enough, that the aggressive animal will become docile. Some breeders say that the spayed bitch will become fat, lazy, and lethargic. According to the records that have been kept on bitches following the spaying operation, such is not the case. It is unjust to accuse the spaying operation when really the dog's owner is at fault—he just feeds the dog too much.

THE CASTRATION OF DOGS

This operation consists of the complete removal of the testes. Ordinarily the operation is not encouraged. Circumstances may attenuate the judgment, however. Castration may be necessary to correct certain pathological conditions such as a tumor, chronic prostatitis, and types of perineal troubles. Promiscuous wetting is sometimes an excuse for desexing.

It must be remembered that as with the spayed bitch, the castrated dog is barred from the show ring.

ANAL GLANDS

On either side of the anus of the dog is situated an anal gland, which secretes a lubricant that better enables the dog to expel the contents of the rectum. These glands are subject to being clogged, and in them accumulates a fetid mass. This accumulation is not, strictly speaking, a disease—unless it becomes infected and purulent. Almost all dogs have it, and most of them are neglected without serious consequences. However, they are better if they are relieved. Their spirits improve, their eyes brighten, and even their coats gradually grow more lively if the putrid mass is occasionally squeezed out of the anus.

This is accomplished by seizing the tail with the left hand, encircling its base with the thumb and forefinger of the right hand, and pressing the anus firmly between thumb and finger. The process results in momentary pain to the dog and often causes him to flinch, which may be disregarded. A semi-liquid of vile odor is extruded from the anus. The operation should be repeated at intervals of from one week to one month, depending on the rapidity of glandular accumulation. No harm results from the frequency of such relief, although there may be no apparent results if the anal glands are kept free of their accumulations.

If this process of squeezing out of the glands is neglected, the glands sometimes become infected and surgery becomes necessary. This is seldom the case, but, if needful at all, it must be entrusted to a skillful veterinary surgeon.

111

METRITIS

Metritis is the acute or chronic inflammation of the uterus of the bitch and may result from any one of a number of things. Perhaps the most common factor, especially in eight- to twelve-year-old bitches, is pseudocyesis, or false pregnancy. Metritis often follows whelping; it may be the result of a retained placenta, or of infection of the uterus following the manual or instrument removal of a puppy.

The term pyometria is generally restricted to cases where the uterus is greatly enlarged and filled with pus. In most such cases surgery must be resorted to in order to effect a cure.

SIDING
TONGUE &
GROOVE

ASSEMBLED VIEW

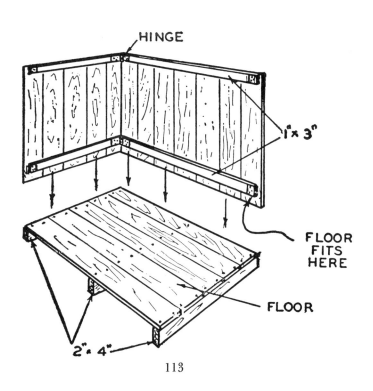

HINGE

1" x 3"

FLOOR
FITS
HERE

FLOOR

2" x 4"

113

Housing for Dogs

EVERY owner will have, and will have to solve, his own problems about providing his dog or dogs with quarters best suited to the dog's convenience. The special circumstances of each particular owner will determine what kind of home he will provide for his dogs. Here it is impossible to provide more than a few generalities upon the subject.

Little more need be said than that fit quarters for dogs must be secure, clean, dry, and warm. Consideration must be given to convenience in the care of kennel inmates by owners of a large number of dogs, but by the time one's activities enlarge to such proportions one will have formulated one's own concept of how best to house one's dogs. Here, advice will be predicated upon the maintenance of not more than three or four adult dogs with accommodations for an occasional litter of puppies.

First, let it be noted that dogs are not sensitive to aesthetic considerations in the place they are kept; they have no appreciation of the beauty of their surroundings. They do like soft beds of sufficient thickness to protect them from the coldness of the floors. These beds should be secluded and covered to conserve body heat. A box or crate of adequate size to permit the dog to lie full length in it will suffice. The cushion may be a burlap bag stuffed with shredded paper, *not straw, hay, or grass.* Paper is recommended, for its use will reduce the possibility of the dog's developing skin trouble.

Most dogs are allergic to fungi found on vegetative matter such as straw, hay, and grass. Wood shavings and excelsior may be used with impunity.

The kennel should be light, except for a retiring place; if sunshine is available at least part of the day, so much the better. Boxes in a shed or garage with secure wire runs to which the dogs have ready access suffice very well, are very inexpensive, and are easy to plan and to arrange. The runs should be made of wire fencing strong enough that the dogs are unable to tear it with their teeth and high enough that the dogs are unable to jump or climb over it. In-turning flanges of wire netting at the tops of the fences tend to obviate jumping. Boards, rocks, or cement buried around the fences forestall burrowing to freedom.

These pens need not be large, if the dogs are given frequent respites from their captivity and an opportunity to obtain needed exercise. However, they should be large enough to relieve them of the aspect of cages. Concrete floors for such pens are admittedly easy to keep clean and sanitary. However, they have no resilience, and the feet of dogs confined for long periods on concrete floors are prone to spread and their shoulders to loosen. A further objection to concrete is that it grows hot in the summer sunshine and is very cold in winter. If it is used for flooring at all, a low platform of wood, large enough to enable the dogs to sprawl out on it full length, should be provided in each pen.

A well drained soil is to be preferred to concrete, if it is available; but it must be dug out to the depth of three inches and renewed occasionally, if it is used. Otherwise, the accumulation of urine will make it sour and offensive. Agricultural limestone, applied monthly and liberally, will "sweeten" the soil.

Gates, hinges, latches, and other hardware must be trustworthy. The purpose of such quarters is to confine the dogs and to keep them from running at large; unless they serve such a purpose they are useless. One wants to know when one puts a dog in his kennel, the dog will be there when one returns. An improvised kennel of old chicken wire will not suffice for one never knows whether it will hold one's dogs or not.

Frequently two friendly bitches may be housed together, or a dog housed with a bitch. Unless one is sure of male friendships, it is seldom safe to house two adult male dogs together. It is better, if possible, to provide a separate kennel for each mature dog. But, if the dogs can be housed side by side with only a wire fence between them, they can have companionship without rancor. Night barking can be controlled by confining the dogs indoors or by shutting them up in their boxes.

Adult dogs require artificial heat in only the coldest of climates, if they are provided with tight boxes placed under shelter. Puppies need heat in cold weather up until weaning time, and even thereafter if they are not permitted to sleep together. Snuggled together in a tight box with shredded paper, they can withstand much cold without discomfort. All dogs in winter without artificial heat should have an increase of their rations—especially as pertains to fat content.

Whatever artificial heat is provided for dogs should be safe, foolproof, and dog-proof. Caution should be exercised that electric wiring is not exposed, that stoves cannot be tipped over, and that it is impossible for sparks from them to ignite the premises. Many fires in kennels, the results of defective heating apparatus or careless handling of it, have brought about the deaths of the inmates. It is because of them that this seemingly unnecessary warning is given.

No better place for a dog to live can be found than the home of its owner, sharing even his bed if permitted. So is the dog happiest. There is a limit, however, to the number of dogs that can be tolerated in the house. The keeper of a small kennel can be expected to alternate his favorite dogs in his own house, thus giving them a respite to confinement in a kennel. Provision must be made for a place of exercise and relief at frequent intervals for dogs kept in the house. An enclosed dooryard will serve such a purpose, or the dog may be exercised on a lead with as much benefit to the owner as to the dog.

That the quarters of the dog shall be dry is even more important than that they shall be warm. A damp, drafty kennel is the cause of much kennel disease and indisposition. It is harmless to permit a dog to go out into inclement weather of his own choice, if he is provided with a sheltered bed to which he may retire to dry himself.

By cleanness, sanitation is meant—freedom from vermin and bacteria. A little coat of dust or a degree of disorder does not discommode the dog or impair his welfare, but the best dog keepers are orderly persons. They at least do not permit bedding and old

116

bones to accumulate in a dog's bed, and they take the trouble to spray with antiseptic or wash with soap and water their dog's house at frequent intervals. The feces in the kennel runs should be picked up and destroyed at least once, and better twice, daily. Persistent filth in kennels can be counted on as a source of illness sooner or later. This warning appears superfluous, but it isn't; the number of ailing dogs kept in dirty, unsanitary kennels is amazing. It is one of the axioms of keeping dogs that their quarters must be sanitary or disease is sure to ensue.

GOOD DOG KEEPING PRACTICES

Pride of ownership is greatly enhanced when the owner takes care to maintain his dog in the best possible condition at all times. And meticulous grooming not only will make the dog look better but also will make him feel better. As part of the regular, daily routine, the grooming of the dog will prove neither arduous nor time consuming; it will also obviate the necessity for indulging in a rigorous program designed to correct the unkempt state in which too many owners permit their dogs to appear. Certainly, spending a few minutes each day will be well worth while, for the result will be a healthier, happier, and more desirable canine companion.

THAT DOGGY ODOR

Many persons are disgusted to the point of refusal to keep a dog by what they fancy is a "doggy odor." Of course, almost everything has a characteristic odor—everyone is familiar with the smell of the rose. No one would want the dog to smell like a rose, and, conversely, the world wouldn't like it very well if the rose smelled doggy. The dog must emit a certain amount of characteristic odor or he wouldn't be a dog. That seems to be his God-given grant. However, when the odor becomes too strong and obnoxious, then it is time to look for the reason. In most cases it is the result of clogged anal glands. If this be the case, all one must do to rid the pet of his odor is to express the contents of these glands and apply to the anal region a little soap and water.

If the odor is one of putrefaction, look to his mouth for the trouble. The teeth may need scaling, or a diseased root of some

117

one or two teeth that need to be treated may be the source of the odor. In some dogs there is a fold or a crease in the lower lip near the lower canine tooth, and this may need attention. This spot is favored by fungi that cause considerable damage to the part. The smell here is somewhat akin to the odor of human feet that have been attacked by the fungus of athlete's foot.

The odor may be coming from the coat if the dog is heavily infested with fleas or lice. Too, dogs seem to enjoy the odor of dead fish and often roll on a foul smelling fish that has been cast up on the beach. The dog with a bad case of otitis can fairly "drive you out of the room" with this peculiar odor. Obviously, the way to rid the dog of odor is to find from whence it comes and then take steps to eliminate it. Some dogs have a tendency toward excessive flatulence (gas). These animals should have a complete change of diet and with the reducing of the carbohydrate content, a teaspoon of granular charcoal should be added to each feeding.

BATHING THE DOG

There is little to say about giving a bath to a dog, except that he shall be placed in a tub of warm (not hot) water and thoroughly scrubbed. He may, like a spoiled child, object to the ordeal, but if handled gently and firmly he will submit to what he knows to be inevitable.

The water must be only tepid, so as not to shock or chill the dog. A bland, unmedicated soap is best, for such soaps do not irritate the skin or dry out the hair. Even better than soap is one of the powdered detergents marketed especially for this purpose. They rinse away better and more easily than soap and do not leave the coat gummy or sticky.

It is best to begin with the face, which should be thoroughly and briskly washed with a cloth. Care should be taken that the cleaning solvent does not get into the dog's eyes, not because of the likelihood of causing permanent harm, but because such an experience is unpleasant to the dog and prone to prejudice him against future baths. The interior of the ear canals should be thoroughly cleansed until they not only look clean but also until no unpleasant odor comes from them. The head may then be rinsed and dried before proceeding to the body. Especial attention should be given to the drying of the ears, inside and outside. Many ear infections arise from failure to dry the canals completely.

With the head bathed and the surplus water removed from that part, the body must be soaked thoroughly with water, either with a hose or by dipping the water from the bath and pouring it over the dog's back until he is totally wetted. Thereafter, the soap or detergent should be applied and rubbed until it lathers freely. A stiff brush is useful in penetrating the coat and cleansing the skin. It is not sufficient to wash only the back and sides—the belly, neck, legs, feet, and tail must all be scrubbed thoroughly.

If the dog is very dirty, it may be well to rinse him lightly and repeat the soaping process and scrub again. Thereafter, the dog must be rinsed with warm (tepid) water until all suds and soil come away. If a bath spray is available, the rinsing is an easy matter. If the dog must be rinsed in standing water, it will be needful to renew it two or three times.

When he is thoroughly rinsed, it is well to remove such surplus water as may be squeezed with the hand, after which he is enveloped with a turkish towel, lifted from the tub, and rubbed until he is dry. This will probably require two or three dry towels. In the process of drying the dog, it is well to return again and again to the interior of the ears.

THE DOG'S TEETH

The dog, like the human being, has two successive sets of teeth, the so-called milk teeth or baby teeth, which are shed and replaced later by the permanent teeth. The temporary teeth, which begin to emerge when the puppy is two and a half to three weeks of age, offer no difficulty. The full set of milk teeth (consisting usually of six incisors and two canines in each jaw, with four molars in the upper jaw and six molars in the lower jaw) is completed usually just before weaning time. Except for some obvious malformation, the milk teeth may be ignored and forgotten about.

At about the fourth month the baby teeth are shed and gradually replaced by the permanent teeth. This shedding and replacement process may consume some three or four months. This is about the most critical period of the dog's life—his adolescence. Some constitutionally vigorous dogs go through their teething easily, with no

119

seeming awareness that the change is taking place. Others, less vigorous, may suffer from soreness of the gums, go off in flesh, and require pampering. While they are teething, puppies should be particularly protected from exposure to infectious diseases and should be fed on nutritious foods, especially meat and milk.

The permanent teeth normally consist of 42—six incisors and two canines (fangs) in each jaw, with twelve molars in the upper jaw and fourteen in the lower jaw. Occasionally the front molars fail to emerge; this deficiency is considered by most judges to be only a minor fault, if the absence is noticed at all.

Dentition is a heritable factor in the dog, and some dogs have soft, brittle and defective permanent teeth, no matter how excellent the diet and the care given them. The teeth of those dogs which are predisposed to have excellent sound ones, however, can be ruined by an inferior diet prior to and during the period of their eruption. At this time, for the teeth to develop properly, a dog must have an adequate supply of calcium phosphate and vitamin D, besides all the protein he can consume.

Often the permanent teeth emerge before the shedding of the milk teeth, in which case the dog may have parts of both sets at the same time. The milk teeth will eventually drop out, but as long as they remain they may deflect or displace the second teeth in the process of their growth. The incisors are the teeth in which a malformation may result from the late dropping of the baby teeth. When it is realized just how important a correct "bite" may be deemed in the show ring, the hazards of permitting the baby teeth to deflect the permanent set will be understood.

The baby teeth in such a case must be dislodged and removed. The roots of the baby teeth are resorbed in the gums, and the teeth can usually be extracted by firm pressure of thumb and finger, although it may be necessary to employ forceps or to take the puppy to the veterinarian.

The permanent teeth of the puppy are usually somewhat overshot, by which is meant that the upper incisors protrude over and do not play upon the lower incisors. Maturity may be trusted to remedy this apparent defect unless it is too pronounced.

An undershot mouth in a puppy, on the other hand, tends to grow worse as the dog matures. Whether or not it has been caused by the displacement of the permanent teeth by the persistence of the milk teeth, it can sometimes be remedied (or at least bettered) by frequent hard pressure of the thumb on the lower jaw, forcing the lower teeth backward to meet the upper ones. Braces on dog teeth have seldom proved efficacious, but pressure and massage are worth trying on the bad mouth of an otherwise excellent puppy.

High and persistent fevers, especially from the fourth to the ninth month, sometimes result in discolored, pitted, and defective teeth, commonly called "distemper teeth." They often result from maladies other than distemper. There is little that can be done for them. They are unpleasant to see and are subject to penalty in the show ring, but are serviceable to the dog. Distemper teeth are not in themselves heritable, but the predisposition for their development appears to be. At least, at the teething age, the offspring from distemper toothed ancestors seem to be especially prone to fevers which impair their dentition.

Older dogs, especially those fed largely upon carbohydrates, tend to accumulate more or less tartar upon their teeth. The tartar generally starts at the gum line on the molars and extends gradually to the cusp. To rectify this condition, the dog's teeth should be scaled by a veterinarian.

The cleanliness of a dog's mouth may be brought about and the formation of tartar discouraged by the scouring of the teeth with a moist cloth dipped in a mixture of equal parts of table salt and baking soda.

A large bone given the dog to chew on or play with tends to prevent tartar from forming on the teeth. If tartar is present, the chewing and gnawing on the bone will help to remove the deposit mechanically. A bone given to puppies will act as a teething ring and aid in the cutting of the permanent teeth. So will beef hide strips you can buy in pet shops.

CARE OF THE NAILS

The nails of the dog should be kept shortened and blunted right down to the quick—never into the quick. If this is not done, the toes may spread and the foot may splay into a veritable pancake. Some dogs have naturally flat feet, which they have inherited. No pretense is made that the shortening of the nails of such a foot will obviate the fault entirely and make the foot beautiful or serviceable.

It will only improve the appearance and make the best of an obvious fault. Short nails do, however, emphasize the excellence of a good foot.

Some dogs keep their nails short by digging and friction. Their nails require little attention, but it is a rare dog whose foot cannot be bettered by artificially shortening the nails.

Nail clippers are available, made especially for the purpose. After using them, the sides of the nail should be filed away as much as is possible without touching the quick. Carefully done, it causes the dog no discomfort. But, once the quick of a dog's nail has been injured, he may forever afterward resent and fight having his feet treated or even having them examined.

The obvious horn of the nail can be removed, after which the quick will recede to permit the removal of more horn the following week. This process may be kept up until the nail is as short and blunt as it can be made, after which nails will need attention only at intervals of six weeks or two months.

Some persons clip the nails right back to the toes in one fell swoop, disregarding injury to the quick and pain of the dog. The nails bleed and the dog limps for a day or two, but infection seldom develops. Such a procedure should not be undertaken without a general anesthetic. If an anesthetic is used, this forthright method does not prejudice the dog against having his feet handled.

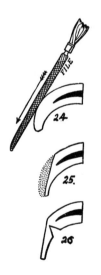

NAIL TRIMMING ILLUSTRATED

The method here illustrated is to take a sharp file and stroke the nail downwards in the direction of the arrow, as in Figure 24, until it assumes the shape in Figure 25, the shaded portion being the part removed, a three-cornered file should then be used on the underside just missing the quick, as in Figure 26, and the operation is then complete, the dog running about quickly wears the nail to the proper shape.

122

Care for
the Old Dog

FIRST, how old is old, in a dog? Some breeds live longer than others, as a general rule. The only regularity about dog ages at death is their irregularity breed to breed and dog to dog.

The dog owner can best determine senility in his canine friend by the dog's appearance and behavior. Old dogs "slow down" much as humans do. The stairs are a little steeper, the breath a little shorter, the eye dimmer, the hearing usually a little harder.

As prevention is always better than cure, a dog's life may be happily and healthfully extended if certain precautionary steps are taken. As the aging process becomes quite evident, the owner should become more considerate of his dog's weaknesses, procrastinations and lapses. A softer, drier, warmer bed may be advisable; a foam rubber mattress will be appreciated. If a kennel dog has been able to endure record-breaking hot or cold, torrential or desert-dry days, he may in his old age appreciate spending his nights at least in a warm, comfy human house. And if the weather outside is frightful during the day, he should—for minimum comfort and safety—be brought inside before pneumonia sets in.

The old dog should NOT be required or expected to chase a ball, or a pheasant, or one of his species of different sex. The old bitch should not continue motherhood.

If many teeth are gone or going, foods should be softer. The diet should be blander—delete sweet or spicy or heavy tidbits—and there should be less of it, usually. The older dog needs less fat, less carbohydrate and less minerals unless disease and convalescence dictate otherwise. DON'T PERMIT AN OLD DOG TO GET FAT! It's cruel. The special diet known as PD or KD may be in order, if the dog has dietary troubles or a disease concomitant with old age. The veterinarian should be asked about PD or KD diets. Vitamin B-12 and other vitamin reinforcements may help.

The dog diseases of old age parallel many of the human illnesses. Senior male dogs suffer from prostate trouble, kidney disease and cancer. Senior bitches suffer from metritis and cancer. Both sexes suffer blindness, deafness and paralysis. Dogs suffer from heart disease; I know one old dog that is living an especially happy old age through the courtesy of digitalis. If the symptoms of any disease manifest themselves in an old dog the veterinarian MUST be consulted.

Many dog owners are selfish about old dogs. In their reluctance to lose faithful friends, they try to keep their canine companions alive in terminal illnesses, such as galloping cancer. If the veterinarian holds little or no promise for recovery of a pet from an illness associated with old age, or if the pet suffers, the kindest act the owner can perform is to request euthanasia. In this sad event, the kindest step the owner may take in *his* interest is to acquire a puppy or young dog of the same breed immediately. Puppies have a wonderful way of absorbing grief!

Glossary of Dog Terms

Achilles tendon: The large tendon attaching the muscle of the calf in the second thigh to the bone below the hock; the hamstring.

A.K.C.: The American Kennel Club.

Albino: An animal having a congenital deficiency of pigment in the skin, hair, and eyes.

American Kennel Club: A federation of member show-giving and specialty clubs which maintains a stud book, and formulates and enforces rules under which dog shows and other canine activities in the United States are conducted. Its address is 51 Madison Ave., New York, N. Y. 10010.

Angulation: The angles of the bony structure at the joints, particularly of the shoulder with the upper arm (front angulation), or the angles at the stifle and the hock (rear angulation).

Anus: The posterior opening of the alimentary canal through which the feces are discharged.

Apple head: A rounded or domed skull.

Balance: A nice adjustment of the parts one to another; no part too big or too small for the whole organism; symmetry.

Barrel: The ribs and body.

Bitch: The female of the dog species.

Blaze: A white line or marking extending from the top of the skull (often from the occiput), between the eyes, and over the muzzle.

Brisket: The breast or lower part of the chest in front of and between the forelegs, sometimes including the part extending back some distance behind the forelegs.

Burr: The visible, irregular inside formation of the ear.

Butterfly nose: A nose spotted or speckled with flesh color.

Canine: (Noun) Any animal of the family *Canidae,* including dogs, wolves, jackals, and foxes.
(Adjective) Of or pertaining to such animals; having the nature and qualities of a dog.

Canine tooth: The long tooth next behind the incisors in each side of each jaw; the fang.

Castrate: (Verb) Surgically to remove the gonads of either sex, usually said of the testes of the male.

Character: A combination of points of appearance, behavior, and disposition

125

contributing to the whole dog and distinctive of the individual dog or of its particular breed.

Cheeky: Having rounded muscular padding on sides of the skull.

Chiseled: (Said of the muzzle) modeled or delicately cut away in front of the eyes to conform to breed type.

Chops: The mouth, jaws, lips, and cushion.

Close-coupled: Short in the loins.

Cobby: Stout, stocky, short-bodied; compactly made; like a cob (horse).

Coupling: The part of the body joining the hindquarters to the parts of the body in front; the loin; the flank.

Cowhocks: Hocks turned inward and converging like the presumed hocks of a cow.

Croup: The rear of the back above the hind limbs; the line from the pelvis to the set-on of the tail.

Cryptorchid: A male animal in which the testicles are not externally apparent, having failed to descend normally, not to be confused with a castrated dog.

Dentition: The number, kind, form, and arrangement of the teeth.

Dewclaws: Additional toes on the inside of the leg above the foot; the ones on the rear legs usually removed in puppyhood in most breeds.

Dewlap: The pendulous fold of skin under the neck.

Distemper teeth: The discolored and pitted teeth which result from some febrile disease.

Down in (or on) pastern: With forelegs more or less bent at the pastern joint.

Dry: Free from surplus skin or flesh about mouth, lips, or throat.

Dudley nose: A brown or flesh-colored nose, usually accompanied by eye-rims of the same shade and light eyes.

Ewe-neck: A thin sheep-like neck, having insufficient, faulty, or concave arch.

Expression: The combination of various features of the head and face, particularly the size, shape, placement and color of eyes, to produce a certain impression, the outlook.

Femur: The heavy bone of the true thigh.

Fetlock or Fetlock joint: The joint between the pastern and the lower arm; sometimes called the "knee," although it does not correspond to the human knee.

Fiddle front: A crooked front with bandy legs, out at elbow, converging at pastern joints, and turned out pasterns and feet, with or without bent bones of forearms.

Flews: The chops; pendulous lateral parts of the upper lips.

Forearm: The part of the front leg between the elbow and pastern.

Front: The entire aspect of a dog, except the head, when seen from the front; the forehand.

Guard hairs: The longer, smoother, stiffer hairs which grow through the undercoat and normally conceal it.

Hackney action: The high lifting of the front feet, like that of a Hackney horse, a waste of effort.

Hare-foot: A long, narrow, and close-toed foot, like that of the hare or rabbit.

Haw: The third eyelid, or nictitating membrane, especially when inflamed.

Height: The vertical distance from withers at top of shoulder blades to floor.

Hock: The lower joint in the hind leg, corresponding to the human ankle; sometimes, incorrectly, the part of the hind leg, from the hock joint to the foot.

Humerus: The bone of the upper arm.

Incisors: The teeth adapted for cutting; specifically, the six small front teeth in each jaw between the canines or fangs.

Knuckling over: Projecting or bulging forward of the front legs at the pastern joint; incorrectly called knuckle knees.

Leather: Pendant ears.

Lippy: With lips longer or fuller than desirable in the breed under consideration.

Loaded: Padded with superfluous muscle (said of such shoulders).

Loins: That part on either side of the spinal column between the hipbone and the false ribs.

Molar tooth: A rear, cheek tooth adapted for grinding food.

Monorchid: A male animal having but one testicle in the scrotum; monorchids may be potent and fertile.

Muzzle: The part of the face in front of the eyes.

Nictitating membrane: A thin membrane at the inner angle of the eye or beneath the lower lid, capable of being drawn across the eyeball. This membrane is frequently surgically excised in some breeds to improve the expression.

Occiput or occipital protuberance: The bony knob at the top of the skull between the ears.

Occlusion: The bringing together of the opposing surfaces of the two jaws; the relation between those surfaces when in contact.

Olfactory: Of or pertaining to the sense of smell.

Out at elbow: With elbows turned outward from body due to faulty joint and front formation, usually accompanied by pigeon-toes; loose-fronted.

Out at shoulder: With shoulder blades loosely attached to the body, leaving the shoulders jutting out in relief and increasing the breadth of the front.

Overshot: Having the lower jaw so short that the upper and lower incisors fail to meet; pig-jawed.

Pace: A gait in which the legs move in lateral pairs, the animal supported alternatively by the right and left legs.

Pad: The cushion-like, tough sole of the foot.

Pastern: That part of the foreleg between the fetlock or pastern joint and the foot; sometimes incorrectly used for pastern joint or fetlock.

Period of gestation: The duration of pregnancy, about 63 days in the dog.

Puppy: Technically, a dog under a year in age.

Quarters: The two hind legs taken together.

Roach-back: An arched or convex spine, the curvature rising gently behind the withers and carrying over the loins; wheel-back.

Roman nose: The convex curved top line of the muzzle.

Scapula: The shoulder blade.

Scissors bite: A bite in which the incisors of the upper jaw just overlap and play upon those of the lower jaw.

Slab sides: Flat sides with insufficient spring of ribs.

Snipey: Snipe-nosed, said of a muzzle too sharply pointed, narrow, or weak.

Spay: To render a bitch sterile by the surgical removal of her ovaries; to castrate a bitch.

Specialty club: An organization to sponsor and forward the interests of a single breed.

Specialty show: A dog show confined to a single breed.

Spring: The roundness of ribs.

Stifle or stifle joint: The joint next above the hock, and near the flank, in the hind leg; the joint corresponding to the knee in man.

Stop: The depression or step between the forehead and the muzzle between the eyes.

Straight hocks: Hocks lacking bend or angulation.

Straight shoulders: Shoulder formation with blades too upright, with angle greater than 90° with bone of upper arm.

Substance: Strength of skeleton, and weight of solid musculature.

Sway-back: A spine with sagging, concave curvature from withers to pelvis.

Thorax: The part of the body between the neck and the abdomen, and supported by the ribs and sternum.

Throaty: Possessing a superfluous amount of skin under the throat.

Undercoat: A growth of short, fine hair, or pile, partly or entirely concealed by the coarser top coat which grows through it.

Undershot: Having the lower incisor teeth projecting beyond the upper ones when the mouth is closed; the opposite to overshot; prognathous; underhung.

Upper arm: The part of the dog between the elbow and point of shoulder.

Weaving: Crossing the front legs one over the other in action.

Withers: The part between the shoulder bones at the base of the neck; the point from which the height of a dog is usually measured.

(End of Part II. Please see Contents page for total number of pages in book.)